Girl Walks into a Bar...

GOTHAM
BOOKS

RACHEL DRATCH

Girl Walks into a Bar...

Comedy Calamities,
Dating Disasters, and a Midlife Miracle

GOTHAM BOOKS

Published by Penguin Group (USA) Inc.
375 Hudson Street, New York, New York 10014, U.S.A.
Penguin Group (Canada), 90 Eglinton Avenue East, Suite 700, Toronto, Ontario
M4P 2Y3, Canada (a division of Pearson Penguin Canada Inc.); Penguin Books
Ltd, 80 Strand, London WC2R 0RL, England; Penguin Ireland, 25 St Stephen's
Green, Dublin 2, Ireland (a division of Penguin Books Ltd); Penguin Group
(Australia), 250 Camberwell Road, Camberwell, Victoria 3124, Australia (a
division of Pearson Australia Group Pty Ltd); Penguin Books India Pvt Ltd,
11 Community Centre, Panchsheel Park, New Delhi–110 017, India; Penguin
Group (NZ), 67 Apollo Drive, Rosedale, Auckland 0632, New Zealand (a
division of Pearson New Zealand Ltd); Penguin Books (South Africa) (Pty) Ltd,
24 Sturdee Avenue, Rosebank, Johannesburg 2196, South Africa

Penguin Books Ltd, Registered Offices: 80 Strand, London
WC2R 0RL, England

Published by Gotham Books, a member of Penguin Group (USA) Inc.

First printing, May 2012
2 4 6 8 10 9 7 5 3 1

LIBRARY OF CONGRESS CATALOGING-IN-PUBLICATION DATA
Dratch, Rachel.
Girl walks into a bar— : comedy calamities, dating disasters,
and a midlife miracle / Rachel Dratch.
p. cm.
ISBN 978-1-59240-711-8
1. Dratch, Rachel.   2. Women comedians—United
States—Biography.   I. Title.
PN2287.D5495A3 2012
792.702'8092—dc23
[B]

2011047377

Printed in the United States of America
SET IN NEW CLEAR ERA
DESIGNED BY JUDITH STAGNITTO ABBATE/ABBATE DESIGN

While the author has made every effort to provide accurate telephone numbers
and Internet addresses at the time of publication, neither the publisher nor
the author assumes any responsibility for errors, or for changes that occur after
publication. Further, the publisher does not have any control over and does not
assume any responsibility for author or third-party websites or their content.

For Eli,

Beyond my imagination

This book starts off by talking about Showbiz for a while, but I assure you, it is actually not about Showbiz. It's about Not Showbiz, and what happened to my life when Not Showbiz became my un-chosen profession. . . .

Prologue

"Hey, I know you!" said the stranger.

I was on Third Ave in New York, emerging from the Starbucks.

"Hi," I said.

The stranger turned to his friend and nudged him. "You know who that is? *SNL! SNL*, man!"

The friend gave a vague, fake nod of recognition. The stranger tried to convince his friend to be more excited.

"She's *funny*!" He turned back to me. "What's your name again?"

"Rachel."

"Yeahhhh! Rachel! Man! *SNL! SNL!*"

The friend looked down the street, wanting to move on.

"Awwww! I miss seeing you on TV! I never see you in movies or anything anymore!" said the stranger.

"Yeah, well . . ."

"What happened to you?!"

• • •

How to answer this question: What happened to me? Where have I been since you last saw me on TV? *I* know where I've been. My friends know where I've been. They see me all the time. But, to the comedy-viewing public—*Where have I been?* Sometimes people think I'm still working, because they see me on reruns of *Saturday Night Live* or *King of Queens.* People think if they see you on reruns, that means you're working. No. You are sitting in your apartment watching Judge Mathis. That's what you are doing.

Don't get me wrong. I'm still a vibrant part of the showbiz community. My agent still calls with offers for work. It goes like this:

RRRIIIINNG! RRRIIIINNG!

"Yay!" I think to myself. "It's my agent!"

"Hi, Rachel. Is this a bad time?"

"No, not at all!" I hit TiVo to pause Judge Mathis. He is about to deliver a verdict to the girl being sued by her mother for wrecking her car.

"We've got an offer for you."

"An offer. Great!" An offer means you don't have to go in and audition—the part is yours if you want it. It's my lucky day.

"It's to play the part of Cammy."

"That sounds awesome!"

"It shoots in November for two days."

"Great!"

"Cammy is the lesbian friend of the two leads."

"OK!"

"Now, in the script it says she's three hundred pounds, but just ignore that."

"Uh-huh."

"You have three lines."

"Hmm. Um. Can I think about it?"

"Sure. Give it some thought. I'll circle back."

"OK. Bye."

An hour goes by. I finish up my courtroom duties for the moment and move on to my other career: amateur psychologist with Dr. Phil. I kind of detest him, but I get a secret thrill at how pompous he is. I also love how his wife, Robin, sits in the audience smiling every episode and that's her job. Right now, he's speaking to a mom who is addicted to Oxycontin. *"Now, I'm not gonna tell you that what you're doing is even a little bit OK? 'Cause it's not?"*

RRRIIIINNG! RRRIIIINNG!

No way. It's my agent again!

"Hello?"

"Hey, Rachel. I got another part here."

"Yeah?"

"They want you to come in and read for the part of Ginge."

"OK. That sounds funny; *now* we're getting somewhere."

"So don't get put off by the character description. Keep an open mind."

"Hit me."

"Ginge is the chief of police."

"OK!"

"It says in the script she's a fifty-five-year-old bull dyke. Obese. But they want you to put your spin on it."

"Okaaay. Wow. Fifty-five years old . . . and obese?"

"Well, they say that, but they don't really know what they're looking for."

"You know I'm trying to get away from these kinds of parts, right?"

"Think on it. You might want to just go in and read for it. I'll send you the sides."

"OK. Bye."

Wow. Well. I . . . do . . . not know about this. I return to the television. After Dr. Phil, I may as well head back to the courtroom for Judge Judy. I think of my college classmates from Dartmouth who are performing neurosurgery at this moment, or being senators (Kirsten Gillibrand [D] NY). Coming up on Judge Judy: "'YOU'RE A MORON, SIR!' 'Listen, she told me I could keep her dog.' 'I DON'T WANT TO HEAR IT! I'M SMARTER THAN YOU, SIR! DO YOU UNDERSTAND?' 'Um . . .' 'UM IS NOT AN ANSWER!'"

RRRIIIINNG! RRRIIIINNG!

What the huh? It's my agent again.

"Rachel, I have another part for you."

"Three parts in one day? This is unheard of. It almost seems like it's being used as a comedic device."

"Character is named LaLa."

"OK."

"Now, don't pay attention to what it says in the script. It's a great part and the movie's gonna be huge. Paul Rudd is the lead. You just have one scene, but it's a killer."

"OK."

"LaLa is a mousy secretary."

"OK. That's my specialty. What's the scene?"

"LaLa walks into the room. She's sixty years old. She is the ugliest woman in the world."

"Sorry, wait, I thought you just said she's the ugliest woman in the world."

"Well, that's what it says in the script, but you know, they just write that . . ."

"Oh, man."

". . . and in the movie there's a contest to see how much money each man would pay to not have sex with LaLa. But that doesn't mean they think that about *you*. They want *your* spin on it. It's one day. Pays scale. You have to fly yourself to LA."

"Um, let me call you back."

These are pretty much the only parts I'm offered since I've been off *SNL*. Lesbians. Secretaries. Sometimes secretaries who are lesbians. Usually much older than I am in real life. Usually about 100–200 pounds more than I am in real life.

I am offered solely the parts that I like to refer to as The Unfuckables.

In reality, if you saw me walking down the street, you wouldn't point at me and recoil and throw up and hide behind a shrub. But by Hollywood standards, I'm a troll, ogre, woodland creature, or manly lesbian. I must emphasize that of course in the real world, lesbians come in all shapes, sizes, and varieties of hotness. I'm not talking about the real world—I'm talking about Hollywood and Hollywood comedies, where lesbians come in two varieties—the hot, unattainable, "What?

You're a lesbian? No way! Not after you get with me!" variety, and the mullet-sporters. Needless to say, I was being called in for the latter. It's like how black and Latino actors get frustrated because they're called in only to play drug dealers, or Arab actors get calls to play cab drivers and terrorists. In the narrow lens of Hollywood, which wants to give the instant stereotype viewers can zone into, I belong in the lesbian parts. Trolls, ogres, and woodland creatures can be done with CGI, so that leaves yours truly to play the bull dykes.

That's the very quick answer to the question "What happened to me?" But read on—I'll tell you some more.

We're Going in
a Different Direction

📺

I was a cast member on *Saturday Night Live* for seven years. Then my contract was up. I was going to be starring in a new show called *30 Rock* in the role of Jenna. Have you guys seen *30 Rock*? Yeah . . . I'm not Jenna.

That was back in 2006 and strangers *still* ask me, "Why aren't you on *30 Rock*?" "What happened with *30 Rock*?" "Are we gonna see you on more *30 Rock*?"

30 Rock. If you are one of those "Oh! I don't have a *television*" people, then I will give you a brief background. Of course, if you don't have a television, then none of the following will matter to you, but let me tell you, *this* is the *very important* stuff you are missing while you are playing the fiddle or telling stories by firelight or whatever it is you do instead of watching TV. *30 Rock* is a show about the backstage happenings at an *SNL*-type comedy show called *The Girlie Show*. Created by and starring Tina Fey. Produced by Lorne Michaels (who, for you actively non-TV people, is also the creator and producer of *Saturday Night Live*). Also starring Alec Baldwin and four other actors Tina had worked with previously—Tracy Morgan from *SNL*, Jack McBrayer and Scott Adsit from Second City, and, briefly, me from both *SNL* and Second City.

After we shot the pilot, I got a call from my agent. "They're changing the show." Or he may have said, "They're going in a different direction." In showbiz, you hear that phrase a lot. At best, it means you are being replaced by a black man. ("Oh! I couldn't have done that part—now it's about a black man! The character of Suzie is now named Jamal! See? They went in a *Different Direction*!!") At worst, the different direction is the direction of Away From You, as in "We Don't Much Care for You!"

At the time, I was not even upset by this news. I was told that the show, which in the pilot had included real sketches within the context of the sitcom, was now no longer going to have sketches. Instead of a sketch performer, they wanted more a sitcom ingénue type. If you have been in the acting business for any length of time, you don't take this stuff personally. Replacements in pilots happen all the time. Everyone always refers to the fact that Lisa Kudrow was replaced on *Frasier*—"and look what happened to her! She went on to do *Friends*!" It's the anecdote that always gets trotted out of the barn whenever an actor is consoling another for being kicked off a job. Besides, Tina called me up and said that, instead of Jenna, she had thought up a different role for me to play. Actually, many roles. I would appear in various episodes as a different character each time, popping up in the show in all sorts of incarnations. I thought this idea was unique. I had never seen anything like it before, and I thought it could be fun to be a sort of "Where's Waldo?" character within the show. Plus, I felt way more comfortable doing these kinds of parts than playing Jenna, a diva type who, in the pilot, sort of tries to seduce Alec Baldwin. No one needs to see me try to seduce. I think that would be grim and awkward for all parties involved. I felt fine about the whole situation. And then things started to go in a Different Direction.

For one thing, this story became instantly public. Before, I had a mild level of fame—not the type to land me in a blurb in *Vanity Fair*—"spotted dining in one of New York's hotspots, Rachel Dratch had the duck confit!" But after I got replaced on the pilot by Jane Krakowski, oh boy, was I a celebrity! I had never been *this* mentioned in the press or *this* buzzed about for my whole career, until now that something "bad" was happening. "Someone's getting fired? Tell me everything. Now, who is Rachel Dratch again?" It was everywhere—"What a Downer for Dratch" read the articles, and here's where the story turns ugly. Literally.

The general opinion seemed to be that it wasn't about "sitcom" or "sketch." It was about attractiveness. It was about Pretty. The Internet, magazines, and news stories all gingerly speculated that I had been replaced by a more attractive actor and that this was the *only* reason I had been replaced.

Well, the newspapers and magazines did so gingerly. There is nothing "gingerly" about the Internet. When I first got hired on *SNL*, I was warned by the other actors: Don't read what they say about you on the Internet. With newfound fame, that's like telling a child, "Whatever you do, don't look behind this door." My fellow cast member Ana Gasteyer would call the act of reading people's comments about yourself on the Internet "cutting," as in the mental illness of cutting yourself with sharp objects. She'd come in and say, "I cut last night." Occasionally, you would look online if you were feeling masochistic. Early in my *SNL* career, I stopped pretty much for good when I saw one comment that hit me in the face like a frying pan. Actually, that was the comment. It said I looked as if I had been hit in the face by a frying pan.

I arrived on the *30 Rock* set to play my first little character. Because I still had a part on the show, I was in the unique situation of being there for the reshoot of the pilot I had shot a few months earlier. Most actors replaced on pilots aren't then hanging around to see how all the action goes down when they no longer have the part. "No matter, I'm a professional!" I thought. As I walked onto the set of the "backstage area" and rounded the bend, it occurred to me I might need more than professionalism. I might need superhuman Zen master strength: There, surrounding me, were these huge pictures of Jane Krakowski posing as various characters in the posters for *The Girlie Show*. There was Jane dressed as a little girl with a huge lollipop! There she was as a grumpy old lady clutching her purse! In a way, the posters were no surprise; I had seen them before. They were exact duplicates of the posters I had posed for when we shot the pilot earlier in the summer and *I* was Jenna—same setups, same poses and looks and props. They were everywhere and they were large. Was this real or was I having some sort of fun-house mirror/showbiz anxiety dream?

Later that day, the surreal feeling continued. The first character I was playing was the Cat Wrangler—a woman who was based on all the animal wranglers Tina had encountered on various sets. The Cat Wrangler was not an attractive lady. Working with all those cats, she was not dressed for glamour, and she had a long mullet. Bad clothes, no makeup, and horrible hair. Lesbian? Check!

At this read-through, there was a video feed to the big NBC execs over in Burbank, so we were all seated around this horseshoe-shaped table. That way, the people in California could watch the performance of the script as it occurred. In an unfortunate coincidence, it just so happened that the producers in New York wanted to see how my wig and costume looked *right* when it was time for the read-through to begin. There I was at the table—the *only* one in costume, and everyone else looking fresh as a daisy. Jane was in some hottie dress with regular-person makeup; all the guys were in their regular clothes; Tina was there, looking cute. And pan across the table to the end aaaand . . . AGH! Who is that person in the corner with the wiry mullet? The one who looks like a carnie worker in the army jacket? That must be Rachel. Whoo, boy. We really made the right decision there, guys. I imagined them high-fiving over in Burbank as I tried to shrink myself into my own mullet to provide maximal invisibility.

To her credit, Jane made things much easier early on when we were in the makeup room. She stated outright, "This is really awkward," and I agreed and that was that. I was relieved that we addressed our strange circumstance. I should point out that we had this conversation while she was wearing a showgirl costume—a showgirl costume exactly like the one I had worn for the pilot, the costume that may well have been a factor in my losing the part, for I'm sure I looked quite comical in it, and Jane looked like a hot showgirl.

Oh, Lord. At least my first week on the job led me to a deep and soul-affirming conclusion, a lesson I could carry with me as I traveled the peaks and valleys of life's journey: Showbiz be crazy.

Luckily, after that first week, my anxiety dream ended, and I started to feel more comfortable on the set. I was having fun playing my various characters—one week I'd be Liz Taylor, another a little blue man who was Tracy's hallucination, another a Polish hooker. And Jane immediately made the part of Jenna her own, defining her as the wacky diva she would be known for as the show developed. Off the set, though, people kept asking about what had happened: strangers on the street when I was going to get coffee, relatives at a holiday when I was just trying to relax with my fourth glass of wine, casual red-carpet interviewers I thought were going to ask me an inane thing like "What are you going to be for Halloween?!" who would instead suddenly decide to go all *60 Minutes* on me—"SO WHAT HAPPENED WITH *30 ROCK*?!" As the questions kept coming, I found myself starting to waver between the two theories of why I had been recast. More often I had the more sane and pro-Rachel opinion that it was just a case of type, that they wanted an ingénue and not a sketch performer.

When I was younger and in acting class in high school or college, we didn't really understand type. In class, I could be playing Lady Macbeth or Blanche DuBois—terribly, mind you—but we were taught that acting is all about becoming the character and drawing on your own personal experiences to embody the character's situation. You can do anything! At Second City or even *SNL*, it worked the same way, only in a comic context—I could play a supermodel in a sketch at Second City, or the president, or . . . well, whatever I wanted! In a sketch show, your own personal type doesn't really matter; your talent lies in the fact that you can play all sorts of character types. When you get to sitcomland, or movieland, though, your own type is a factor. I'm not going to play a hottie on TV when real hotties exist . . . superhotties that moved to LA from their small towns in Iowa because they were born superhotties.

In terms of my type, I knew I was no leading lady or diva. I always thought I would end up in that typical "best friend" role in movies or TV, but it would turn out that, by Hollywood standards, I was too odd to play even that. Especially nowadays—the best friend is someone *slightly* less beautiful than the leading lady, except with brown hair. Or glasses! "Hey! She's wearing glasses! My brain now sees her as slightly less attractive than the lead! Everything makes sense in the world!" That's the reality I was beginning to comprehend. That's Hollywood, kids (I say as I take a drag of my More lady cigarette). It ain't all glitz and glamour and shrimp cocktail and cocaine parties.

In my less self-assured moments, the more negative speculation about the replacement started to seep into my head. Maybe all those meanies on the Internet were right; maybe a bunch of focus groups watched the pilot and checked off a box marked "No!" Maybe the way it works for a new show is a bunch of TV execs sit around a room with some wires and EKGs attached to their wangs, and when I was on screen, the needle dipped dangerously into the Code Red Anti-Boner Zone. I was starting to feel like the ten years of training and performing and sweating it out pre-*SNL*, plus the seven years *at SNL*, all went out the window because I didn't have a symmetrical face. This would have been OK if at some point along the way I had gotten the memo: "Oh, and if you want to be a successful female comedian, you better have a symmetrical face." Maybe I was naïve, but this was the first I was hearing of it. I grew up watching perfectly lovely female performers whom I don't think you would call "hotties": Gilda Radner, Lily Tomlin, Carol Burnett. Those were my comedy idols. I would think of the genius Jean Stapleton of *All in the Family* and how today some ding-dong in the network would insist she be played by Megan Fox to get the male 18–49 demographic. "People," he'd say at the meeting, "Megan can be *very* funny." I had always been pretty sure that comedy was about producing a laugh and not a boner. Now I had to produce laughs *and* boners? When did the rules change? This is not the kind of stuff you consider when you are young and dreaming about becoming an actor and thinking, "I have fun doing the school plays!"

SHOW!!!!!!

A moment of early showmanship with my aunt Susan.
Not pictured in this photo: my jazz hands.

The setting: A suburban living room, Lexington, Massachusetts

The year: 1975

The Event: A Choreographed Dance to Rosemary Clooney's "The Kitty Kat's Party" That Will Rock Your Freaking World

As we look back in history, this is the first known official Rachel Dratch Production that we find in our extensive research. Not only did I serve as choreographer, I was also performer, casting director, publicist, and costume designer.

(Those ears and tails weren't going to make themselves.) I suppose as I listened to the strains of Rosemary Clooney over and over again on my 78 rpm record (I just lost everyone under the age of forty with that reference), a creative vision began forming in my nine-year-old head, a vision that could not be denied. Yes, the Kitty Kat's Party must be enacted through the art of The Dahnce. My younger brother and a few neighborhood kids were enlisted to enact said Kitty Kats, to fulfill my Artistic Vision. I believe the lyrics went "At the kitty kat's party, all the kittens will be there, they'll be dressed up in their Sunday best with flowers in their hair." If memory serves, the dance consisted of some minor hand gestures and cat motions, nothing too strenuous . . . no lifts. And lip-synching. To wrassle up an audience, check out how cute/pathetic this is: I went to the little farm-stand store across the street from my house and put up a homemade sign that simply said *"SHOW!!!!!!"* with my home address and the date and time. The cost of admission, I believe, was twenty-five cents, really a lot of entertainment on the dollar when you think about it. And at the bottom, the sign said *"All proceeds go to Muscular Dystrophy"* because at the time, everyone was having those McDonald's "carnivals" in their backyards for muscular dystrophy. (Of course, to a kid, finding out that the carnival consisted of a huge vat of orangeade and a beanbag toss was heartbreaking when you were picturing a Ferris wheel magically set up in your neighbor's backyard.) Needless to say, no proceeds were raised for muscular dystrophy through my production. The audience consisted solely of our parents, but I didn't mind. Any sucka who wasn't in the audience that day missed out on quite a SHOW!!!!!!

Soon after this, I met with my first big success in a wider arena. No, I was not cast as one of the orphans in the national tour of *Annie*, though that was surely my fantasy. My fifth-grade teacher, Miss Nancy Tokarz, was a big proponent of creative writing. She had us do a ton of it that year. This is notable because pretty much all my English classes after that were just about reading a great work of literature and commenting on it. She was one of the only teachers I recall in my entire education who focused on creating a story rather than commenting on one. We were assigned to write a story, and one of the stories would be picked to be produced as a play—live on stage! My story was picked and thus, my first work, "Autobiography of a Leaf," was brought to the masses (and by masses I mean some parents in a gymnasium in Lexington, MA). It was about a leaf who lives through the winter, told, as the title suggests, from the point of view of the talking leaf. Pretty heady stuff. There I was, the narrator, with a green leaf/sandwich board as my costume. When I said, "And then autumn came," I turned the leaf so the back was now the front, and I went from green to orange. The audience responded. My first big laugh.

• • •

By this time, I had already started watching *Saturday Night Live*, during its very first season. Though my parents were young and hip, I didn't find *SNL* through them. I discovered *SNL* the way I discovered all things adult and semi-forbidden: through my friend Jill. It was Jill who told me how babies were made that same year, for though my parents were, as I said, young and hip, Jill's parents were young, hip, and far more open. Jill was seeing R-rated movies like *Jaws*, whereas my first R-rated movie was still years away. Although I was jealous of her adult status, when she got home from seeing the movie with her parents, she did throw up. I guess being on the fast track has its drawbacks.

Along with introducing me to the world of sex and shark attacks, Jill was also my liaison to *Saturday Night Live*. The first time I saw the show, I was sleeping over at her house, and her older brother, Mark, was watching it. Older siblings were scary to me. I was the oldest kid in my family and when faced with a friend's older sibling, I would skulk around and be very deferential. There was Mark in their living room watching *SNL*, and we plopped down on the floor and started watching it too. I remember being immediately fascinated. What was this secret world I had just stumbled upon? It had a feeling like nothing I'd ever seen on TV. I remember thinking it was really funny, but I also knew full well that half of the jokes were going over my nine-year-old head.

I started watching the show of my own accord every week. If I had a friend sleep over, we would watch *The Love Boat*, then

Fantasy Island, and then *SNL*. My friends were never all that interested in *SNL*. I'd feel responsible if one of the sketches was incomprehensible to us. I'd try hard to telepathically send out the vibes to my hapless friends: "Just stick with it!" They would invariably fall asleep partway through, but I would watch the whole thing—I was always a night owl, even back then. My favorites were Lisa Loopner, the Coneheads, Roseanne Roseanna Danna, the Wild and Crazy Guys, Mr. Bill—all the stuff even a kid could understand. I thought "Samurai Delicatessen" was really funny, but I wasn't quite sure what was happening. The Bees—well, I didn't get that at all, but I still don't now, so I'm going to give myself a pass on that one. I remember one week, a musician named David Bowie performed wearing a dress. I didn't have an explanation for my sleepover friends for this one, either. I had no idea that years later I would be in that very studio, getting my head shot taken for my opening credit, and that David Bowie would be the musical guest for my very first show. While my picture was being taken for my dream job, David Bowie was right there rehearsing with his band, singing "Rebel Rebel." This time he wasn't in a dress, though.

I didn't grow up thinking, "I want to be an ACTRESS!" I thought it seemed like it would be really fun, but it seemed too crazy a dream to have. I did have comedy all around me as a child. My parents loved Johnny Carson, Mel Brooks, *SNL*, Woody Allen, and the Three Stooges° (°Dad only). My father was and still is an exceptionally funny guy. He was particularly good at doing imitations. The baby of the family, he was a typical youngest kid—attention-seeking and the life of the party.

My mom has a creative wit of her own, often put to use in writing funny poems for people's birthdays, and she served as a good straight man to my dad—"Oh, Paaauuul!" she'd say when he'd start to get what she deemed too unruly. My younger brother, Dan, was in on the action as well, making up goofy songs in the backseat of the car on road trips. He ended up going into comedy too, as a TV writer. The funny thing is, my brother and I weren't marching around the house saying, "We're gonna be in COMEDY!" It just kind of happened because of the sense of humor that was floating around, I suppose. I was at a girl's house during high school, and her father

Halloween, 1976—My brother and I show an early affinity for the comedy world: Dan is the Unknown Comic from The Gong Show, *and I am a Conehead. (Can you tell I made my own costume?)*

happened to be a high school classmate of my father. He told me, "Your dad was always imitating the teachers as soon as they left the room!" I had no idea he did that as a kid, but I was busy doing the same thing.

Throw into this mix my group of funny girlfriends, many of whom I'd known since elementary school, who only added to my burgeoning class clown status. I would pipe up with one-liners from my seat in junior high. As I grew older, I still didn't seriously think of trying to become a professional actor, yet I kept doing plays. I went to summer theater camp four years in a row, which I think officially qualifies me as a drama geek. Though I hung out on weekends with jocks and the group who would go drink in the woods (not so unlike Sully and Denise, the sketch I would do on *SNL*), during the school week, I'd be puttin' on the ol' "character shoes" to rehearse for the high school musical. (Fellow drama geeks will back me up—those Capezio character shoes signified you meant business and probably knew the lyrics to "Out Here on My Own" from *Fame* by heart.) Even so, acting was just a hobby to me, and besides, I was off to a prestigious college where I'd probably end up becoming a professional of some sort, perhaps a psychologist, I was thinking. I had no idea my choice of college would send me running into the world of comedy.

WASP World

Ḃ

The year was 1984, and I, an eighteen-year-old Jewish
girl from suburban Boston, was arriving at my new campus,
Dartmouth College, where I was about to encounter a species of
human I had never met in my life. I speak of the WASP. Not just
one WASP, a swarm of WASPS: blond and beautiful women
wearing pearls, and the daughters of oil barons from Texas. Gorgeous adolescent males from Deerfield and Exeter who looked
as if they'd walked off the pages of a J.Crew catalog. The *Dartmouth Review*, a super-right-wing college newspaper, had a big
voice on campus. Laura Ingraham, the ultraconservative com-
mentator, was a vocal student there and she was heading up the
Review, along with future speechwriters for George Bush, such
as Dinesh D'Souza. The following year, members of the *Review*
would destroy the antiapartheid shanties that had been con-
structed on the green. Wait a minute! What was I doing here in
this hotbed of right-wing delights? Like many seventeen-year-
olds looking at schools, my main criterion had been "This is a
pretty campus!" Plus, every student I met seemed to love the

place with a devotion usually reserved for a cult. Walking around the campus as a prospective student, I was sucked in, seeing all the dreamy, perfect-looking boys who looked like they were straight out of a teen movie. When I got there, I eventually realized that the guys who look like that in movies are usually the antagonists to the goofy underdogs whom everyone's rooting for—the campus had its fair share of James Spaders from *Pretty in Pink*, Neidermeyers from *Animal House*, and faux Neidermeyers from *Revenge of the Nerds*. I think I would have been happier in college with the Duckies, the Blutos, and the Nerds, and in spite of its academic reputation, back in the eighties, there weren't many Nerds at Dartmouth.

I got my first glimpse of what a culture shock college would be on my very first Dartmouth experience—the freshman trip. These are hiking and camping trips you take before school starts, to get into the groove and supposedly have fun. I signed up for the easiest, level-1 trip because I'm a terrible athlete. Upon meeting my fellow freshman-trippers, I discovered that the most beautiful girl I had ever seen was in my group. This chick was total Dartmouth material. She was named Abigail and was a natural-blond species the likes of which did not exist in my high school. Although she was perfectly friendly and nice to me, I took one look at her and was like, "Oh, nooo! I think I picked the wrong school!" When I was eighteen, I didn't have the faith in myself to listen to my gut feeling. I don't mean to say that I saw one beautiful girl and freaked out—it was the *type* of beautiful girl: the confidence, the breeziness, the probable lineage connecting her to the *Mayflower*. Oh, and as a side note, she was doing our level-1 trip on *crutches* because she had sprained her ankle being a champion tennis player. Otherwise, she would have been on a real hiking trip. You should have seen the guys fighting to carry her over the streams.

I had come from my hometown public high school with my funny friends and Irish and Italian characters, and here I was with people who had last names for first names, like Farnsworth and Chadwell. Where were the Sullys? The Smittys? (They were at UMass or Plymouth State.) Now, I know it's not like I was coming from the ghet-to. My town, back then, was about a third Irish, a third Italian, and a third Jewish, and our parents were largely second generation who had managed to move out to the burbs. Overall, I felt quite comfortable in high school. All had been rosy in my world, or, as some people from my high school might say, everything was wicked pissah.

For this next section, if you happen to have a cassette tape of REM's "Murmur" lying around, throw it into your boom box, which you also surely have on hand, and press PLAY, because that was the sound track I had on constant loop for much of my time at Dartmouth, where I was feeling none of the comfort level I had in high school. I was rejected from the two plays I auditioned for during the fall and winter trimesters. I thought I really might have had a shot in the winter— they were doing William Inge's *Picnic* and I was auditioning to play Millie, the more plain younger sister of the beautiful Madge. (Madge, no joke, was played by Freshman Trip Abigail.) As I was walking onto the stage to audition, the director said of the girl who had just auditioned before me, "Well, I think we found our Millie!"

The Greek system was huge at Dartmouth and though I never aspired to be in a sorority, it seemed like "Everyone's doin' it!" so I went ahead and rushed. I was not invited back to any sororities after the first round of rush. Lest you think I had social issues, this one really baffled me, because making friends had never been a problem for me. I think I was wearing the wrong dress—a little corduroy number. Yes, I was rocking a corduroy dress, with long sleeves, that I thought was cute but clearly was all wrong. I felt as if I had now been literally cast out to match the general figurative outcast feeling I already had there. In addition, I was also rejected by the damn *Freshman Cabaret*—a little medley of dumb sketches and stuff that anyone who'd ever set foot on a stage, or even never set foot on a stage and just had some general enthusiasm, could be in! You can see how I may not have been feeling in tip-top form. Oh, and I was also rejected from the a cappella singing group the Decibelles (!), but that rejection I'm sure I deserved. Throw into this mix that I had a roommate who was, um, let's call it "making love" to anything that moved, at rates that made me wonder if she was going for some sort of plaque above the large fireplace in the student center. I was on the other end of the spectrum, pure as the Hanover snow, which was probably still about five feet high in April.

After a summer of being back home working as a bus boy at the Magic Pan in the Burlington Mall (Do you remember the Magic Pan? Home of that newfangled eighties delicacy, the *crepe*! It's what passed for exotic French food in the world of the suburbs), I returned to Dartmouth for sophomore fall to discover that I had a bad lottery number for housing, so I had to move from my old-school, beautiful, centrally located ivy-covered dorm down to a faraway land called the River Cluster—an ugly group of seventies-looking cinder-block towers that was the equivalent of Siberia. No one hung out at the River Cluster. You just went there to sleep. I had been assigned a roommate, but she somehow escaped, and as a measure of how depressed I was to be there, I never even moved my stuff into her larger area of the room. I stayed in my tiny side of the room and did nothing with the larger part, which could have been turned into some sort of fun living area, I suppose, but that would mean you'd have to somehow lure people down to the River Cluster, which wasn't going to happen. As I said, I was starting to feel depressed, something I hadn't experienced previously, so much so that I worked up my courage to go to the school counselor. I was really nervous about it. This meant I actually had a *problem*. I no longer had the ability to keep fooling myself that I liked this place.

I walked into the counselor's office and had another instant gut feeling. I took one look at this guy and was like, "Nope!" I wanted some hip, young *warm* person that I would feel comfortable talking to. I had never been to a counselor. I didn't know what to expect. Out walked a man who was older than my dad, with gray balding hair, a powder-blue sweater, and the neutral expression passed down from generation upon generation of the salt-of-the-earth, granite-in-your-veins New Englanders. At the time, though, with my lack of belief in my instincts, a subtle thought merely wafted through my brain—almost like a scene from *Invasion of the Body Snatchers*, a tiny voice said, "He's one of them!"

The counseling session was completely fruitless. I think I said something to the effect that I was just not finding anyone here that I liked, that this wasn't my scene and I was thinking of transferring. He would respond only by asking me about my family and kept trying to dig around with an "Is everything OK at home?" tactic. "YES! EVERYTHING'S GREAT AT HOME!" I wanted to shout back. "THAT'S THE PROBLEM! Sully's there! And Smitty! And I think I was happier working at the Magic Pan!" That may sound strange since I was fortunate enough to be at this esteemed campus, but when you aren't happy, you aren't happy, and the detriments were vastly outweighing the blessings.

I was still thinking of transferring. I think I had gone so far as to pick up some applications for other schools, and that's when, during my sophomore winter, I saw the Dartmouth improv group perform. "Ooh!" I thought. "I could do that!" I had always gravitated toward comedy in theater anyway. I got to sit in on one of their rehearsals through a friend from acting class. They invited me to join the group, which was called Said and Done, and it was my salvation. Finally, I had found some people who enjoyed looking foolish and were a bit offbeat and were definitely funny and creative.

Improvisation was the perfect branch of acting for me—it's perfect for those who don't like to prepare, or, as one might also call them, the *lazy*. There are rules to improv that can help you be a better improviser, but you don't have to study for a test or rehearse a monologue. You don't have to "find your moments" or learn your lines. You are *in* your moment and you make up your *own* lines. If you are any good, your lines are

My college improv group doing that mainstay piece of beginning improvisers: the Machine!

funny. And they are funnier than anything you could have thought of if you were sitting staring at a computer (back then, that was the Mac 128k) trying to think up some comedy.

At one of the first Said and Done rehearsals I attended, I experienced that thing that happens in improv, when the line comes out of your mouth before your brain has registered what you are about to say. We were doing some sort of group poem about money or something, and I said, "I'm so rich that it's no surprise, when I'm tired, I get Gucci bags under my eyes." Now, I'm not saying that is the most brilliant line ever, but hey, I was nineteen years old and I hadn't experienced the phenomenon before. "How did I think of that?" I wondered. I didn't feel like I *had* thought of it. It's a sort of flow that happens when you are completely in the moment and not getting in your own way. Not *trying* so hard, not planning ahead, just getting out of your own head and letting the magic happen. You could apply this to any activity, of course. You could apply it to life.

The biggest rule of improv is called "Yes And." Basically, this means that whatever your scene partner says to you, you agree and then add to it. So if you are starting a scene and your partner says, "I made you a birthday cake, Grandma!" you don't respond, "I'm not your Grandma, and that's not a cake—it's an old shoe!" You would get a quick laugh, but you would kill the reality of the scene entirely. A "Yes And" exchange would be: "I made you a birthday cake, Grandma!" "Oh, thank you, dear. I feel thirty-five years young!" By agreeing to what your partner laid out and adding to it, you've established a relationship and even given your partner something to play with—that this family has a grandmother who is thirty-five years old—and the scene can develop from there. "Yes And" would serve me well, not only onstage but offstage too. Without my realizing it, "Yes And" would contribute to one major career success and one major life event far down the road from the rehearsal room in Hanover, New Hampshire, during the winter of my sophomore year.

Chicago:
Overnight Success in Ten Years!

By the time I graduated, I had ferreted out a group of friends who are still a part of my life to this day. I ended up meeting a lot of my Dartmouth friends through the theater department. Then there's another branch of my guy friends at Dartmouth who all came out of the closet in rapid succession after graduation. (This would begin my long-standing tradition of always having a fab group of gay men to hang with at a moment's notice.) I knew I didn't want to go through life thinking, "What if I had tried to become an actor?" I decided I at least wanted to give it a shot. I had no idea *how* to go about giving acting a shot, though. There was no set plan like it seemed all my classmates had who were applying to med school or law school or going into the corporate world. My improv group had done an exploratory trip to Chicago over the summer to check it out, and I decided to move there after graduating to try to get into the improv comedy mecca of the country, the Second City.

I remember sitting in my packed car, about to leave my parents' house, thinking, "I'll be back in a year and then I can go to grad school and become a therapist." I drove out with Sonja, a girl from my improv group. Sonja was a bit of an eccentric and would be one of the two people I knew in Chicago, in addition to being my roommate. Just to give you a little snapshot of Sonja: One time, a friend was sitting next to her in class, where she observed Sonja feel something that was stuck in her tights. Sonja, thinking no one was watching, worked the object up her leg and somehow retrieved it out of the waistband of her tights, whereupon she discovered the object was a raisin. She then ate it.

Back in Massachusetts, as we packed up my car to set off on our journey, one of the items Sonja loaded into my Honda was a bag of flour. I mean, what if they didn't have flour in Chicago? It lasted the whole trip, until we pulled up in Chicago, she opened the door to get out, and it exploded all over my car. She would go on to eventually become a professor of theater at the University of Minnesota.

I began my professional comedy career with an instant bomb to the ego, when Sonja and I both auditioned for classes at Second City, and Sonja got in and I did not. We had heard that getting into the classes was a mere formality. *Anyone* with *any* improv experience gets into the classes. That's what we had heard. I had been in Chicago for two weeks and wondered if I should get back into my flour-covered car and drive home to Massachusetts.

Needless to say, I didn't. I stayed. I did some plays. I took some classes elsewhere and got into the Second City classes later that year. I also started at Improvolympic, where I "studied" under the esteemed improv guru, Del Close. I would go watch the house team, Blue Velveeta, perform every single weekend, which was a good way to learn by osmosis. After two years in Chicago, I auditioned for the Second City touring company and . . . I had instant success and was off on my path to the top like the rising star that I was? No. I did not get into the touring company on my first try. I did get in the following year, on the second try. This became my pattern—again and again. Ol' Two-Time Dratch, they used to call me. No, they didn't.

The touring company of Second City was certainly not a glamorous gig, but everyone in it was excited because it was the first step to getting onto the mainstage someday. Well, I shouldn't say everyone was excited, because there was always someone in the tourco who'd been touring for several years and was waiting for their break and was embittered and had had it with the road. Eventually, that could be you. But for now, freshly hired, you are excited. Occasionally, you would get to go somewhere really desirable: Alaska, New Orleans, and the coveted "ski tour," on which you perform in all these ski resort towns in Colorado and Utah. More often, though, the tour entailed a seven-hour drive in a van to go to Upper Michigan or Lower Bumdiddle, Indiana. We'd perform at colleges (fun), town events (could be fun), and corporate gigs, where we'd change the lines of the scenes to accommodate the company: "Why, that's almost as funny as *Jerry Harrison's golf game!*" (Thunderous inside-joke-recognition applause.) We got paid sixty-five bucks a show back then. I ended up touring for two and a half years. Finally, after being passed over the first time to move up out of tourco (another "second try"), I got on the mainstage, where I performed eight shows a week for almost four years.

The Second City started up in Chicago in 1959 and, in the early days, produced such esteemed alumni as Fred Willard, Joan Rivers, Alan Arkin, and Peter Boyle. Second City eventually became a feeder to *SNL*: John Belushi, Bill Murray, and Chris Farley all came out of Second City Chicago. Out of the Toronto branch of SC came Dan Aykroyd, Gilda Radner, and Martin Short. The shows at Second City are mainly sketch comedy, like *SNL* sketches, with some improv thrown in. After the show every night but Friday, there's an improv set in which the cast gets suggestions from the audience and just makes stuff up for about a half hour. If an improv scene happens to go really well, the actors in it might make a mental note and remember it for later, to incorporate it into the next written show.

I was there in the early to mid nineties, which felt like a special time to be in Chicago. So many people there ended up being on your TV or movie screens today. While I was in the touring company, on the mainstage were Stephen Colbert, Steve Carell, and Amy Sedaris, all in the same cast. Even back then, Amy Sedaris was this pretty little girl who would screw her face up into the ugliest expressions. I learned a lot from just watching her perform, because she was so fearless and bold in her choices. She wasn't content to be the girly-girl who would play the "Honey!" parts—the trap it was easy for women improvisers to fall into. As in "Honeeyyyyy! I told you to take out the trash!" "Honeeyyyyy! I thought we were going out tonight!!" "Honeeyyyyy! Were you flirting with the waitress?!" (I had learned early on at Improvolympic that it was easy to "cast" yourself into these roles in an improvised scene and let the guys have all the fun. All of the really good women improvisers I knew avoided the "Honey!" parts because it meant they would be relegated to the sidelines of a scene, occasionally stepping in to pour imaginary coffee.) Amy Sedaris would play these little squirrel-like characters and goofy oddballs. Stephen Colbert was the twinkly-eyed, good-looking smarty-pants who actually performed a song about the conflict in the Balkans and managed to make it hilarious. ("We're talkin'! We're talkin'! We're talkin' 'bout the Balkans!") And Steve Carell could make anything funny. I don't think I ever saw him die onstage. In one scene, a couple had a ton of kids, and the cast kept running through the stage, each one playing a different unruly child. Steve Carell simply walked through, holding up a piece of foam mat and said, "I found foam!" and could bring the house down with just that line. Adam McKay, later the head writer of *SNL* and Will Ferrell's writing partner, was with me the whole time from Improvolympic to the mainstage and was always thinking of new ways to do sketch, to screw with the audience and to mess with their heads, or to use comedy to challenge corporate America. I was there just to get some yucks, but he was always thinking with a higher goal in mind. Also on the mainstage with me for two shows: Tina Fey. Amy Poehler was my understudy for the touring company. Horatio Sanz, Nia Vardalos, and many of the eventual writers for Conan O'Brien were at Second City when I was there, as well as a bunch more people you may never have heard of but you should have because there was so much talent going on there in that time. I mention a lot of the people who became famous because you know who they are, but I learned something about comedy from every person I worked with at Second City. Everyone brought their own self to the work, so I was always delighted by my cast mates and laughing along with the audience, wondering, "How'd they think of that?!" Improvising every night after the show, I would sometimes forget I was supposed to go out and participate too because I was so busy laughing at what my fellow performers were doing.

My first year on the mainstage, I remember feeling tentative. The stage was so big, the room was so vast, I was new up there, and it felt like someone else's turf. It took almost a whole year until I felt truly comfortable on that stage, but after that year, I lost much of my fear and hit a whole other zone of improvising. The nightly improvising eventually improved my skills in ways I couldn't imagine. I was able to channel that intangible thing, when you get out of your head, with far greater frequency. Mind you, we'd still bomb occasionally in the improv set, usually when I had a visitor from out of town in the audience. Afterward, I'd sheepishly say, "No, this is usually really funny! I swear!" That was just your run-of-the-mill, every-once-in-a-while, audience-not-laughing-at-all set. Oh, that was child's play, because occasionally there were also the looking-into-your-fellow-performer's-eyes, what-the-hell-is-happening moments. There was the drunk lady wandering onto the stage from the side stage door, just walking right into a scene, trying to participate with her own "lines." We ushered her off the stage only to hear her crashing down the stairs with the sound effect you'd hear in a movie. Then there was the time we were performing a special show for a foundation, and Adam McKay and Scott Adsit were doing a scene called "Gump," wherein Adsit had taken an exam to enter a corporate job and it was discovered that he was legally retarded. The word *retarded* was said about twenty times in this scene. We didn't know it, but the foundation was for developmentally disabled kids, and the poor person who had booked the event had to stand up at intermission and give a speech about how "many people still don't know that the word *retarded* is offensive!" Oh, Lord, and then there was the time when Adam and our director Tom Gianas' "messing with the audience" kick went way out of my comfort zone: Adam and Adsit walked out during the improv set to tell the audience that then-President Clinton had been shot. A gasp rose up from the crowd. Adam and Adsit then wheeled a TV onstage and said we were going to check in on the latest news, and proceeded to play sports bloopers and laugh at them and just wait for the dazed audience to mill out of the room. That was probably my most uncomfortable moment ever on a stage—a time when "Yes And" was stretched to its breaking point for me. But that's risk taking.

Screwing with the audience was never my thing, but those who didn't mind the discomfort became masters and turned it into their own art form. Of course, now that I see the bit in print and I'm not having to live it, it actually sounds kind of funny.

We'd go out pretty much every night after the show to one of two completely smoke-filled bars. We'd often start at the Last Act and then, if it was a really late night, move on to the Old Town Alehouse, which closed at four A.M. . . . five A.M. on Saturdays. We were in our twenties or early thirties and there was no reason not to go out almost every night. On weekends we'd stay until last call, when the bartender, a woman whose name I knew only as Yoyo, would start yelling, "Let's GOOOO, people! Let's GOOOO!" One of the actors, Jerry Minor, became particularly adept at imitating her and could fool people into thinking the bar was closing. People drank and drank, smoked and smoked, and laughed and laughed. You could look around the room and every improviser in the bar was somehow connected to you, because at some point, you'd all shared that unique terror of standing in front of three hundred people and not knowing what you were going to say next.

A lot of people move out to Chicago thinking, "I'll do Second City, and then on to *Saturday Night Live!*" You soon lose your singular *SNL* ambition when you realize *everyone* has this same dream and the odds of actually getting on *SNL* are too slim to hold on to such a specific vision. You also realize that there are many other pathways to make a career in comedy after Second City besides *SNL*. *SNL* would come scouting once in a while but not on any predictable basis. They happened to come right when I had gotten onto the mainstage, but that time, they picked almost every one of the actors to audition (from the mainstage, the E.T.C. stage next door, and the annex stage in the burbs) and I wasn't one of them. By my third and fourth shows on the mainstage, I started to be mentioned in reviews, and I went on to win two Jeff Awards. (That's the Chicago equivalent of the Tonys, so if having a Tony impresses you, dial that reaction down by about 50 percent and bask in my half-glow.) Three years later, I was still on the mainstage, about to leave in two months, and lo and behold, *SNL* came out to scout again. This time, I was picked to go audition for *Saturday Night Live*!

For the *SNL* audition, you create all your own material. The basic guideline is to do three characters and three celebrity impressions. I remember I did my Boston teen character; and a character that never made it onto *SNL*, a former Broadway child star now an adult but still wearing her child-star dress and talking in her child-star voice; and an Eastern European cleaning woman who had been through all these atrocities and now worked in an office where people complained about piddly stuff like bad coffee. I hadn't really done any impressions at Second City—for the audition, I did Calista Flockhart because that's an impression I had randomly come up with while watching *Ally McBeal* in the comfort of my living room. I also did Christiane Amanpour, and as sort of a cheat, I did Madeleine Albright addressing the Teletubbies. I just made a Madeleine Albright face and threw on a Teletubbies voice.

Here's the thing about the audition. They tell you your audition is at three. You get there on time. You can't believe it—you are AUDITIONING FOR *SATURDAY NIGHT LIVE*!!! You are sent to a dressing room. You wait. You wait some more. You wait more. It's now six o'clock. You are finally called in to audition. When you walk into the audition, there are no pleasantries. No "Hi! And what are YOU going to be doing for us? Greeeeat." You just get up on the stage, and a stage manager says, "Five, four, three, two, go." I had been warned that Lorne Michaels and the producers probably wouldn't laugh but not to let that throw me. It happened that because I was the last one of the day, a bunch of people from the office had milled in and were standing in back and they were laughing a lot, which of course helped. When the audition was over, I remembered the whole thing, always a good sign for me. When an audition is a blur afterward, I knew I wasn't good. There was one thing I didn't remember, though. Later I realized, "Oh my God! My audition was on *that stage*! The stage where the host does the monologue! I was standing on the *SNL* stage!"

I felt it could not have gone any better. Whether or not they picked me, at least I knew I had done my best. And . . . I had instant success and was off on my path to the top like the rising star that I was? Nope. Ol' Two-Time Dratch strikes again! I wasn't hired. That year they hired Jimmy Fallon, Horatio Sanz, and Chris Parnell. They told me maybe next year they'd be hiring women, but I let go of the dream, with a genuinely OK feeling about it.

A year later, I did get to audition again. You don't want to go in and do the same stuff you did the year before. I had already used up my best stuff in the previous audition, so now I had to break out "second string" characters. This time I didn't feel quite as good about it. I called up my mom and told her I didn't think I got it. They said they'd let me know by August 15, but I wasn't holding my breath. August 15 came and went without a phone call, and I wasn't too surprised.

Two weeks later, I got a message on my answering machine. (This was 1999, back in the days of answering machines.) "Lorne wants to meet with you in NYC." I flew to New York, sat on the couch outside his office for a few hours, and then had a ten-minute chat with Lorne.

The meeting wasn't any sort of interview situation like "So, what do you hope to bring to the job?" I'm not really sure what we talked about. I remember him telling me that when Candice Bergen would host, Jane Curtin might have less to do that week. It was almost like he was telling me what it would be like if I got to join the cast. And I've heard rumor he has those meetings to make sure you aren't crazy.

My meeting with Lorne in his office ended with him telling me he'd let me know about the job in a week. A week passed. Oh yes, I was counting! And this was the last possible day of "the week." I was walking around with my brand-new cell phone every second of the day (again, 1999, we had all just switched from pagers). There I was, in the shower, the bathroom, Pilates class with my trusty phone. No call. Finally, at six P.M. Los Angeles time—I get THE CALL! "We have Lorne Michaels for you," says a voice on the phone. And there he was.

"Hello, Rachel."

"Hi!"

"I'm up here in Toronto, but someone from NBC will be calling to set up the deal."

"WHAT DOES THAT MEAN!!!?" I'm thinking.

"Um . . . does that mean I got the job?"

Long pause, which probably was actually two seconds.

"Yes."

"Oh! Thank you." (Screaming inside!) "Thank you so much!"

Hang up phone. Scream and jump around. Call parents. Call friends. Scream and jump around some more. Cut to third-grade Rachel getting the news. She screams and jumps around too.

It was ten years almost to the day since I had arrived in Chicago, covered in flour.

Dreams Do Come True!
(And May Be Accompanied
by Debilitating Psychological Torture)

You could probably tell I was the new girl by my unbridled excitement and my unkempt eyebrows. I hadn't touched them before getting hired for *SNL*. What did I know of the importance of brow-shaping to being a lady? At *SNL* I was immediately whisked into a world of excitement and GLAMOUR! I got my photo taken in the studio for the opening credits, and if you recall, David Motherf'ing Bowie was rehearsing with his band and singing "Rebel Rebel." RIGHT THERE! WHILE I WAS GETTING MY PICTURE TAKEN TO BE ON *SATURDAY NIGHT LIVE*!! To this day, I can't hear the song "Rebel Rebel" without thinking of the fact that whatever else happens in life, my gazillion-to-one dream came true.

SNL gives you a month to find your own apartment, so at first I was staying in the Doubletree Suites in Times Square. Times Square is any native New Yorker's most avoided part of the city because of the crowds and the tourists, but of course I didn't mind. I felt like (please say in Liza Minnelli voice) "I'm in New York City! The lights! The crowds! I'm livin' the dream!" Each day I would walk to 30 Rockefeller Plaza, having no idea where the hell I was in the city. I had no orientation of east and west, north and south. I just knew to turn right out of the hotel, and right on Forty-Ninth Street. Oh yes, I was gritty. It was just like Patti Smith.

My first event there was the twenty-fifth anniversary show, and as a new cast member, I would get to sit in the audience. I would be surrounded by every major person who had hosted the show, plus every big musical guest. Any comedy idol I could think of—Steve Martin, Bob Newhart, Bill Murray— was there buzzing around. When I arrived, a producer said, "Where've you been? You have to get in hair and makeup!" What? But I was merely there to sit in the audience! No matter. They had a dress for me to wear, and presented me to Michaelanthony (yes, that is one word), the hairstylist, who gave me a crazy fun 'do. And while I was sitting in the makeup chair, there in the same little room were Lily Tomlin, Dan Aykroyd, and Elvis Costello. This was in-sane.

And then, after that crazy intro to the dream job, here it

was: the very first episode of the season and my national television debut on *Saturday Night Live*! Jerry Seinfeld was the
host. I was going to be playing a child beauty pageant contes-
tant on "Weekend Update." The character was sort of on the
same family tree as the child star I had used for my audition.
My mom came down to watch the show in the live audience.
And the biggest thrill of all—Don Pardo was going to say my
name. I was ready for The! Most! Thrilling! Moment! Of! My!
Life!

The! Most! Thrilling! Moment! Of! My! Life! . . . was going
to have to wait. After dress rehearsal, one of the producers
came into my dressing room and informed me that my piece
was cut. My pink-and-white pageant dress hung on the hook in
my dressing room to punctuate the moment, and to mock me.
In my mind, the piece had gone well, but in this whole new
world, what did I know? I had my first intro to the long tradition of having to answer everyone-you-know's phone calls,
explaining why you didn't appear on the show—in this instance,
on the night of my big debut. I didn't know to give them the
warning that it might not happen. I dusted myself off and was
ready for Week Two.

Week Two! Hosted by Heather Graham! Musical guest
Marc Anthony. Another scene! . . . Cut after dress.

Week Three . . . Hosted by Norm MacDonald! Musical
guests Dr. Dre and Snoop Dogg! And still waiting for The!
Most! Thrilling! Moment! Of! My! Life!

See, what I didn't realize is that Lorne is very careful about
your first appearance on the show. He wants you to really
knock it out of the park and do something that will wow the

audience, not come on with a piece that just goes OK. My child beauty pageant star did just adequately—it didn't *kill*. Finally, on that third show, I got to appear as Calista Flockhart, making the same face I had made screwing around in my living room, only now on national TV. I understood why Lorne made me wait for my debut—I would end up doing that impression many times on the show, and I even got a *Cheers* in *TV Guide* for that first episode. Lorne puts a lot of thought into the show and he is very hands-on with his decisions. He didn't create the show only to delegate and just sit up in some golden tower (although he may well own a golden tower as one of his vacation homes).

I was the only new cast member the season I was hired, and as you can gather, the powers that be don't give you a handbook telling you, "Oh, welcome aboard and here's how everything works!" You are just thrown into the pool—sink or swim. So I will tell you now. This way, if you are ever on *SNL*, you will be prepared. Here it is, reader:

YOUR UNOFFICIAL GUIDE TO BEING ON *SNL*.

THE FIRST STEP is getting your scene on the show. This occurs at the read-through on Wednesday afternoon. You've had virtually no sleep, for you have been up the entire previous night writing. So on Wednesday, the whole cast and the host and Lorne are seated around a giant table, and you all read through or, I should say, perform there at the table, all of the scenes that have been submitted that week. Usually, that's about forty scenes. Virtually every employee of the show is in the room—people from costumes, sets, hair, sound—everyone crammed into the room to hear what possible scenes they may be working on that week. Your scene is read. Sometimes it gets big laughs! Yay! Sometimes it tanks and gets silence. Boooo! By the end of the whole process, the bigwigs—that is, Lorne, a few of the producers, the head writers, and the host—all go behind closed doors and pick which scenes will be in for the week. You hang out in the offices, joke around with cast mates, or drink some wine that has been pilfered from a cabinet somewhere. A few hours later, someone says, "The picks are in!" and you go look at a list, much as you would if you were auditioning for the high school play, to see if your scene has been circled. Sometimes your scene that killed at the table is in! Yay! Sometimes, to your utter dismay, your scene that killed is not in, for reasons that you will never know, so you learn to not even bother asking what went on behind that Great Closed Door. Maybe the male host really wanted to play a woman, so he picked that Hooters scene instead. But that is just your speculation. Often a scene that you found not funny at all is in. Do not question. Someone probably thinks the same about your scene when it gets in. It is all subjective and will make you insane. But this week . . . your scene is in! Yay! Tell all your friends! WAIT!! You soon learn. DON'T TELL ALL YOUR FRIENDS!

There is still a gauntlet to run before you are on TV. You see, Lorne and the producers pick a few more scenes for the dress rehearsal than will make it to the live show. There is a dress rehearsal at eight P.M. on Saturday in front of a live audience, and judging from how your scene goes there, it could still be cut before air. After the dress rehearsal, everyone crams into Lorne's office at about 10:30 P.M. to sit on the floor or a couch arm, and up on a bulletin board the list of scenes that are in is on one side, and the scenes that were cut are on the other side . . . the BAD side!! Some weeks, you are all over the show before dress rehearsal and you walk in to see your three scenes are all on the BAD side of the board, so you end up on the bench that week. But lucky for you, this week, your scene is still in! Yay! Tell all your friends! WAIT!! DON'T TELL ALL YOUR FRIENDS!

You see, gentle reader, your scene is at the end of the show. It's the last scene of the night. Because the show is live, the timing is only an estimate. Quite often, the last scene of the show is cut for time. It's all very frenetic when you find this out. There you are in your chicken suit, excited to do your big chicken scene, and someone runs through the hallway breathlessly saying, "THE CHICKEN SCENE IS CUT!" You dejectedly take off your chicken head. But you still say good nights with your chicken body on, 'cause darn it, someone's going to see and think, "Hey! What's that chicken costume? Oh darn it, that looks really funny! I bet we missed out on a really funny scene there!"

After the show on Saturday night, each cast member gets a limo and you can pile your friends or out-of-town visitors in and head to the party. The parties don't usually get too crazy—they are held in various restaurants around the city, and people sit at the tables with their visitors. The parties serve as the big sigh of relief after all the work that week. Outsiders picture the parties as these debauched crazy affairs with comedians hanging off the chandeliers. That may have been true in the old days, but in my time, looking around the room, you might think the drug of choice was calamari.

As the party winds down for the evening, you ask your friends, "Are you going to the after-after?" The after-after-parties go from around four A.M. until the sun is up, and are held in random dive bars throughout the city. They are a bit more raucous than the after-parties, only because you aren't seated at tables; sometimes there is dancing, and by that hour, people have consumed more alcohol. (My first few years there, I always went to both parties and would stumble home at eight in the morning, sometimes with show makeup still on my face and wig glue still crusted near my ears. Perhaps the most memorable after-after-party was thrown by Tracy Morgan, waaay down at the bottom of Manhattan. We all piled into our cars to go to parts unknown and ended up at a modern apartment building in an area of town I didn't even know existed. Upon entering, we found that interspersed through this party, to serve up cocktails or possibly sexual favors, were stripper ladies who were all of a very specific type. I think whoever organized the party—maybe one of Tracy's cronies?—must have been into short, like five feet tall, Latina ladies of square and stocky build. Each and every lady had the look of an ancient Mayan crammed into black fishnets and garter belts, with red headband tiaras on their heads for extra sexiness. I think I stayed at that party about fifteen minutes, and it served as a tipping point—perhaps I had reached an age when I didn't have to go to *every* after-after-party).

Maybe you had a great show on Saturday and you introduced a new character that was a big hit. Maybe you weren't in the show at all. You have Sunday to bask in your glow or to lick your wounds, because come Monday, the whole process starts all over again, and you better have some new ideas. Oh, and just so you know, the host this week is Christopher Walken, and he's already doing his "Continental" character, and since it's an election year, there's going to be a seven-minute debate sketch, and for some reason, Jay-Z is playing an extra three songs. This all leaves one and a half slots for any new scenes to be picked for the week. Happy Writing! Your unofficial guide is finished! Now fly! Fly, my little comedy star, and I'll see you at the after-party! I'm gonna do a ton of calamari, so if I don't say hi, that's why—I'm gonna be totally f'd up on calamari. Luv n' Kisses, Rachel

The most fun part of *Saturday Night Live* for me was just that—Saturday night and the live show itself. Sometimes people would say, "It's not really live, is it?" YES! It is! It says so right in the title! When you are sitting at home, watching it all on TV, the actor playing the old lady in the scene right before the commercial break who is now an elf when we come back had to transform in those two minutes. If you ever get to see the show live in the audience, then you see that each actor has their own hair, makeup, and wardrobe people, and everyone's running around to get to the next scene. Meanwhile, the sets are being moved around frantically. It's a fascinating operation. And no, I can't get you tickets.

My least favorite night of the week at *SNL* was probably writing night. As I said, everyone stays there all night long, I mean until the sun comes up, and you hope you have an idea that week. As an actor on the show, you have to come up with your own stuff because you can't wait around and hope that a writer will just hand you a fully formed character. That did happen to me a few times, most notably with a creature I played who had an arm coming out of its head. That creature, who—little-known fact—is named Qterplx, was from the mind of writer Scott Wainio and made its first appearance as the illegitimate child of Angelina Jolie and her brother after they shared that kiss at the Oscars. Other than that, for the most part, I thought up my own characters, as was true for the other actors as well.

The *SNL* writing process is a completely different method from Second City's. At Second City, you would have a funny idea, share it with your cast mates, and then improvise in front

of the audience. The scenes were videotaped so you could go back and watch and see what lines really killed and what parts needed to go. For me, improvising always came more naturally, and I could come up with stuff I never would have thought of writing *SNL*-style while staring at a computer screen. I certainly wasn't able to just show up at the *SNL* office, sit at my desk, and think, "Hmm. Let me think up a character that will really resonate with people! It will also resonate enough with Lorne to be picked for the show. Oh, and the host will also love it and want to pick it for the show. And how about a catchphrase that all of America will love to say? This character will recur again and again and again and become a beloved part of *SNL* history! And I'm going to think this up while I'm staring at a blank computer screen and oh-god-I-better-think-of-something-because-I-haven't-been-in-the-show-for-the-past-three-weeks-except-to-play-a-waiter-and-holy-shit-I-have-no-talent-everyone-else-knows-what-they're-doing-AGHHHHH!" Annnd cue peals of laughter coming from the office next door, where people are writing what surely must be the funniest scene ever in the history of comedy. That's what writing night often felt like on a regular basis.

You always knew you were in deep trouble on writing night when you started looking around the room for inspiration. "Hmm. How about a scene about a lamp!? Or what about a plant!?" You were officially toast.

For me, if I was lucky, an idea would pop into my head at a random time and I would save it for the next show. For example, I was once at a party where we were playing the game Celebrity and one of the guests was getting really testy because there was someone on his team who really sucked. So I saved the idea and then the writer Emily Spivey and I wrote a scene based on that, where Eric McCormack was my partner and I got so mad I ended up trashing the whole room and running through the wall Looney Tunes–style. Sometimes a simple joke you are doing with a friend gives you an idea on which to base a whole scene. When Seth Meyers and I were sitting next to each other at read-through, I was using old showbiz terms to joke around about whether a scene would work. I was saying in an old-man Hollywood voice, "Does this scene got legs? *Does it got legs?!*" Seth started saying, "Have you met my agent, Abe Scheinwald?" And we ended up writing it as a scene in which I played old-man Hollywood producer Abe Scheinwald. The best way for me to think up scenes was organically like that.

There were also the characters we actors tried to put up

again and again and just never got on. At this point, I'd like to pour one out for the brothas who never made it, specifically a child star by the name of David Mack Wilson. (I definitely had a thing about wanting to play a child star!) David Mack Wilson is a joke among me and my fellow cast members because, damnit, I tried to get this character on the air again and again, to no avail. He was an obnoxious kid who would go on and on about all his gigs, saying, "Maybe you recognize me from my macaroni 'n' cheese commercial! OK! OK! I'll say it! 'IT'S THE CHEESIEST!'" He'd drive the host crazy with his showbiz tales, saying, "Hey! Ever worked with Hanks? Great guy! How 'bout Hanks and De Niro!? Can you say DREAM PROJECT?!" Anyway, I thought this kid was my next big character but could never get him on. Eventually, he had a walk-on in one episode but didn't turn into the franchise I had imagined. As we would say at *SNL*, David Mack Wilson died of Comedy AIDS. OK, I know that sounds bad, but Comedy AIDS was the disease that claimed the characters who never made it on the air. Hey, I'm just the messenger here.

In many ways, *SNL* is still the greatest job you could ever imagine having as a comedian—just the history, the amazement we all had to be part of this iconic show, the very thought of the comedians who had paved the way there before us, the excitement of the live show, never knowing who might be dropping in that week to do a bit. (Mick Jagger? Martin Short? The Dalai Lama?) The thrill of watching the musical guests rehearse in a semi-empty studio on Thursday afternoons at my own private Bruce Springsteen or U2 concert was surreal.

Here I am back in the day with my SNL *ladies!*

Even if I had only one line in the show that week, I still had the coolest job in the world.

I had some successful recurring characters over the years—the Boston teens Sully and Denise, and one of my personal faves, the Lovers with Will Ferrell—but in my fifth year there, I did the scene that got me the most recognition (cue important-sounding James Lipton voice): I'm talking about Debbie Downer.

> KENAN THOMPSON: *Good morning! Welcome to the Mickey's Breakfast Jamboree! My name is Billiam, and I'll be serving you today. . . . Let me tell you Mickey's specials today. We've got steak and eggs, served with some home fries and Mickey waffles . . .*

JIMMY FALLON: *Ooh! I love me some steak and eggs!*
ME: *Ever since they found mad cow disease in the U.S., I'm
not taking any chances. It can live in your body for years
before it ravages your brain.*
TROMBONE: *WAAAAH WAAAAAAH!*
CUE THEME SONG: *You're enjoying your day, everything's
going your way, then along comes Debbie Downer . . .*

Oh, to have a hit character on *SNL*: the inexact science, the
alignment of the planets to be just so, every cog in the wheel
having to spin precisely right so that the germ of an idea in
your brain can be crafted well enough to make it through the
elaborate process to become reality and be seen by millions,
which propels you into the status of cultural icon for the rest
of history . . . or at least for that week.

The first time we put Debbie Downer on the show, I had a
giggle fit that I couldn't control, and the whole cast ended up
breaking so hard we could never quite recover . . .

HORATIO SANZ: *I'm gonna ride that haunted elevator
thingy. It drops you straight down! . . .*
HOST (LINDSAY LOHAN): *I want to go to every country
in Epcot and greet them in their own native language:
Hola! Konnichiwa! Hi!*
ME: *Did you guys hear about that train explosion in North
Korea?*
All pause and look at me, annoyed.
ME: *The media is so sensitive there . . .* (oops that wasn't
the right word) *so secretive . . .*

I try to stifle a giggle over my flub.

ME, FIGHTING A LAUGH: *That they may never know
how many people perished.*
TROMBONE: *WAAAAH WAAAAAAH!*

Aaaand I break. Accidentally start laughing while camera is in close-up on my face. We all start laughing, never quite regaining control. Audience goes nuts.

People often ask me if Debbie Downer is based on a real person. Well, not really. Although after her creation, I started to notice my mom shares some of her tendencies. I told my mom I was thinking of going to the Dominican Republic for vacation, and she said, "Well, don't wander into Haiti." Oh, believe me, I have repeated the phrase "Don't wander into Haiti" many a time in my family when someone is giving unnecessary safety advice.

In truth, Debbie Downer actually has a rather mystical and personal origin story. The character came about because I took a trip by myself.

I was seeing a therapist who kept insisting that I take a trip alone. (Even though I am a huge fan of therapy to begin with— remember, I originally wanted to *be* a therapist—I will tell you that if you are going to be on *SNL*, you should get a therapist immediately. It's either that or a drinking problem, so take your pick.) Taking a trip by myself was her answer to every problem you could imagine, and most of *my* problems revolved around relationships. If I was afraid I would never meet a guy—"take a trip by yourself." I was dating a jerk—"take a trip by yourself." I'm worried because I don't think I'll ever have kids—"take a trip by yourself." She was an older woman who, in her younger days, had met her husband while traveling alone. Is that what she thought would happen for me? Or would it just force me out of my usual routines and serve as some sort of psychological reset button? I didn't know. It made no sense to me. I really liked to travel, and I had a little gang of ladies to travel with. So why the hell would I want to go somewhere by myself? I was not interested.

Finally, for some reason, she got through to me. I looked at her advice as some sort of "doctor's orders," like taking a pill: I don't know why I'm doing this, I thought, but I'll give it a shot. Even the night before the trip, I was packing, thinking, "What the hell am I doing? This is ridiculous." But I was going. Instead of saying no again and giving the reasons why a trip alone was a bad idea, without consciously realizing it, I had "Yes And"-ed my therapist.

I had picked Costa Rica as my destination because there would be stuff to do there and it wouldn't be me on some beach with a bunch of honeymooning couples. I went to a lodge in the middle of the rain forest. And except for the fact that one night I woke up to find a large beetle halfway up my pajama leg, it was a great trip. I had no idea that I would also get a character out of the deal.

There weren't many people at this lodge, but for meals we sat at communal tables, which was nice because I didn't feel strange being there alone, and it forced me to talk to people.

The surroundings were beautiful: mountains, ocean, monkeys howling in the morning, and scarlet macaws flying overhead. One morning at breakfast, we were just making chitchat and someone asked where I was from. I said, "New York City." And someone else said, "So were you there for 9/11?" The question hung awkwardly in the jungle air and sort of screeched things to a halt. I answered that I was, but sort of tried to get the conversation off the shoulder of the road and back onto the highway. For a week, that moment stayed in my mind just sort of batting around, me thinking nothing of it. When I was back home in New York, I was out listening to a band, something I don't go do very often, and there it was! That bolt from the blue that you hope for—the muses decided to pay me their once-yearly visit. The name Debbie Downer popped into my head, someone who just has to go to the negative stuff that's in all of our heads but that we edit out during a fun moment. I wrote it up that week with the writer Paula Pell. At first we tried to set it in an office, but something just wasn't clicking. Then we realized it needed to be somewhere really happy. And so we set it in Disney World. We started joking around, making that "Waaaah Waaaaaah!" sound while we were writing, and then we thought, "What if we actually put these goofy trombone noises into the scene?" The over-the-top "waaaah waaaaaah"s were making *us* laugh, so we said, "What the hell, let's include them." The scene did well at the read-through table and was picked for the show that week. During rehearsal on Saturday, Jimmy and Horatio were cracking up. "Those guys better knock it off!" I thought. I didn't want them messing with this scene that I felt could actually go pretty well. Of course, on the live show, it was I who ended up cracking up on air, flubbing that one line at the beginning and simply not getting back on track. It was the ultimate "church laugh," where you know you should not be laughing but you can't help yourself. I knew the camera was coming in for a close-up—there was no escaping it by hiding behind another actor or keeping my head down. "GET IT TOGETHER, DRATCH!" I was thinking. "Lorne. Lorne. Lorne. Lorne," I thought. But it was to no avail.

People ask me if Lorne got mad over my giggle fit, and the answer as far as I know is no. The audience eats it up when the actors break during a scene, but I would always try not to break. It can become a cheap tool to get the audience on your side since they dig it so much. I think Lorne knows it's going to happen from time to time, and it's not a big crime on the show. Ironically, although I was being highly unprofessional by laughing so hard through my scene, I think that was my favorite moment of my time on *SNL*. The subsequent Debbie Downer scenes could never hit the heights of that first one with the genuine laughing breakdown. But for me, that first scene was just unbridled joy—we were all having fun and clearly it showed. It also shows just how live the show really is: There are no do-overs, and whatever happens during show-time is out there for all to see. Whether it's because we started laughing in what would become the biggest break-fest in *SNL* history, or because the character resonated with people in an "I know that person!" type of way, I had a hit scene. And it was all because I said yes.

any more questions?

I said this book wasn't about showbiz and so far I've only talked about showbiz. But you have to see where I was coming from before you see where I ended up. So that pretty much wraps up the showbiz section. Oh. Wait . . . no. I see a few hands up in the imaginary crowd of people in my head, wondering about a few things I left out. There are several questions I am asked again and again, so I will close out by answering them. I have to interject that you would be surprised at how often I am asked this stuff by strangers, and that's the only reason I'm going into it here. *I* know that there are far more important issues going on in the world, and that people in France have no idea who I am. Except the Brulés, the French family I lived with for a semester during college. So here are the answers to the last few questions I'm asked a lot. Um, let's see. . . . I see a lot of hands. . . . Yes, you!? Doorman from a few buildings down from my apartment?

"So why aren't you doing those little parts on 30 Rock? *Why aren't you on* 30 Rock *anymore?"*

Well, Manny, my character spots ended up happening less frequently as that first season went on, until the idea was faded off completely when the show returned for its second season. Much as I thought playing the different characters was a cool idea, I could understand the fade-out. New sitcoms are ever-changing beasts, and as the show evolved and the sketch section of the show disappeared, the "Where's Waldo?" thing of me popping up as various characters didn't quite fit in. Also, though Tina made many self-deprecating jokes about low ratings when the show was starting out, *30 Rock* received a great deal of critical acclaim and was developing a reputation as being The Little Cool Show That Could. Big movie stars were starting to do guest spots in the types of parts I would have been playing, movie stars who could bring in more viewers than I to a show that initially was struggling in the ratings. It was kind of a "Well, that's showbiz!" situation.

Tina did have me back to appear on the show a few times as the years went by, for the 100th episode as well as the live episode they did. I liked going back to the set and being able to hang with my old friends and cast mates, well out of the awkward period of the replacement and all the hoopla.

Ok, next question, . . . uh . . . you! My mom's friend from book club? I wanna say your name is Lois?

"Yes. Lois Karshbaum. Weren't you and Tina friends from your Chicago days? Was that weird?"

Well, yes, Lois, Tina and I were friends from back in our Chicago days, and we are still friends now. I have a hunch that my friendship with Tina is one of the reasons my replacement on the pilot got so much publicity. Dozens of actors are replaced on pilots every season, and it's usually a little footnote in a trade paper. Tina and I have been friends for many years, and when you throw in the casting changeup, it makes people wonder—what was *that* like?

Tina and I met in 1996, back in our Second City days in Chicago. I worked with her closely, since we were in two shows on the mainstage together. We did one of my favorite Second City scenes together, a scene called "Wicked" that featured the two of us with thick Boston accents as a mother and daughter shopping at the mall. (It was the precursor to the Boston teens scene we wrote for me and Jimmy Fallon when I landed at *SNL*.) A classic Tina line from "Wicked":

ME: Ma, you're gonna give me a negative body image. You know eight out of ten teenage girls have a negative body image.

TINA: Yeah? Well, six of 'em are right.

We would hang out after the shows, often ending up with her then-boyfriend, now-husband, Jeff, and fellow cast member Scott Adsit at a diner called the Golden Apple. These were the glorious days of one's youth, when you could down a milk shake and French fries at two A.M. without ever gaining weight. Throughout all our time improvising together, up there in front of the Second City audience without a script, Tina and I developed a certain chemistry with each other, a shorthand that has served us over the years. And never did it come in more handy than the time she saved me from exposing myself to an audience of Hollywood bigwigs. I'm not talking about exposing my soul or inner thoughts, I'm talking vaginas here, people.

It all started with the sound of *RRRIIIP*, the loud sound of tearing fabric. I knew that sound could be only one thing . . . 'twas my pants splitting, and as luck would have it, this was the one night of my life that I wasn't wearing underwear. I was standing onstage in front of an audience filled with Hollywood bigwigs, agents, and studio executives at the now-defunct HBO workspace in Los Angeles. Tina Fey and I were performing our two-person sketch show *Dratch and Fey*. We had written and performed the show in Chicago the summer after I moved to LA and she was writing on *SNL*. The following summer, we performed it in New York at the Upright Citizens Brigade Theatre, and it was getting a lot of attention, so we were in LA to show it to industry people there. After I heard the deafening *RRRIIIP* (deafening to me, anyway), I glanced down to see that my pants had split up the *front*, starting at the fly and heading downward. A shot of adrenaline went through my body as a prickly feeling took over the back of my neck. At this point in the show, I was sitting on the floor onstage—that's when my pants had split, when I went to sit on the floor. How bad was it? I looked down again. I saw my own humanity.

Oh my God Oh my God Oh my God. This was a two-person show. There were no breaks. I couldn't run off the stage and somehow fix the problem. Yet how was I going to continue on, with my jive there for the world to see? Prior to the show, in the dressing room with Tina, I had noticed that the pants I was wearing showed panty lines. In New York, doing our show at the Upright Citizens Brigade Theatre, I could have flown with the panty lines. But this was LA! I couldn't have panty lines in LA! So I happened to say to Tina, "I'm just not going to wear underwear." It was a throwaway line. We thought nothing of it.

There onstage in panic mode, I carefully got up off the floor for the next little transition moment of the show, where Tina and I faced each other and danced in a sort of stylized make-out move. Loud music played along, so under the music, I blurted out to her "Ijustsplitmypants." "Grabthatjacket," she said, without missing a beat. There was a sweat jacket on the floor that had been tossed off by one of the characters we had played earlier. I tied it around the front of my pants for the whole rest of the show. No one noticed. Improvisers who perform together for a long time develop a comfort and a trust that if one is floundering, the others will come in and save the moment. Because of our history, I always knew Tina had my back. Now I knew she had my front too.

Point is, Tina and I had both been in the biz long enough to know that some things are beyond our control. When I was replaced on the show, I felt confident that Tina had "fought" for me as much as she saw fit, but that at the same time, the network has certain demands, and the fact exists that I wasn't right for the part as it turned out to be. Oddly enough, I didn't initiate a big Feelings Conversation with her; I didn't want her to think I was expecting her to solve things for me or *fix* anything, especially when she was busy trying to get her show off the ground. She had written me a part in her show (as she did for her old pals Jack McBrayer and Scott Adsit as well), she's always been loyal to her old Chicago gang, and she shows that loyalty with actions big ("You're in my show!") and small ("C'mon over! Jeff's making doughnuts!"). As for the prospect of a big Feelings Conversation, I've never known Tina to be the kind of gal who'd be into putting some Shawn Colvin on the iPod, pulling out an afghan and two mugs of hot cocoa, patting the couch, and saying, "Hey, girlfriend, c'mon over here and let's share our feelings. Mmmm. That's good cocoa." I imagine we would both sign off on the statement that in dealing with feelings, she and I have different styles: I am a classic Pisces, prone to sensitivity and emotions, and she is German.

Well, I see a few more hands up. Yes, lady who I was seated next to at my cousin's wedding?

"Yeah, what's up with 30 Rock!? Why aren't you on 30 Rock anymore?"

Didn't I *just* answer this? Good Lord. Question time is over.

OK! That's the whoooole story of that. Back when it was all going down, I just figured something else would come along and Ol' Two-Time Dratch could chalk this up to the time I lost that one job but then this *other* one happened a little while later. That didn't happen. I'd get some jobs—a day here, a few days there (and at this point I'd like to say I am eternally grateful to Adam Sandler for putting me in his movies)—but no major steady gig as I had pictured happening post-*SNL*. A year passed, then two, then three. All the while, these gnarly parts were mostly all that was coming across the table. The road not taken, being a therapist in the burbs of Boston, was starting to sound like a liberating prospect—not one I was actually considering but a nice little fantasy escape hatch. If I were a therapist, I wouldn't be worried about how my chin looks on camera—or off, for that matter. After all the years of performing, after all the rejections to which I had developed immunity, was I, Rachel, usually a wide-eyed optimist, becoming . . . bitter?

I had to face the facts—I'd had the good fortune of working almost fifteen years straight with a steady gig, but now, for whatever reason, my career was at a standstill. I was no longer Rachel the successful television actor, Rachel the cast member of *SNL*, Rachel the nationally beloved comic treasure. (Was I ever that? Let's just go with it.) No, I was none of those things. I was just me, and how did I feel about being pared down like that? I had to see all the other facets of myself and not hold my identity in acting or comedy. So to fill the day, I began doing all the stuff I'd always wanted to do but never had the time. I took Spanish class. *No puedo hablar pero puedo entendere mejor.* I dog-sat. I did yoga. And then there was The Biggie: After spending years hanging out with cute, flirtatious, comedy non-boyfriends, I was going to find Love. So for starters, I took on the biggest challenge of my life. I tried dating in New York.

Horsemeat

I hadn't gone on many real *dates*: You meet an attractive fellow and hit it off, at which point this debonair man takes control of the situation and says, "Maybe we should continue discussing this . . . over dinner. . . ." In my world, that happens only on my television set.

I've only been in relationships where you meet the guy through whatever it is you're doing, in my case comedy, and then later in the relationship, you find out they are an addict (alcohol, pot, sex—but not with you) and then continue the relationship for about another year. Actual formal "dates," the getting-to-know-you, do-you-like-red-or-white-wine, how-many-brothers-and-sisters-do-you-have dates—I don't know anything about those. At the time I made the decision to go on the Dating Crusade, it had been a long while since I'd had a boyfriend—three years. And I don't even know if I could legitimately call him a boyfriend. . . . He was one of the Three Addicts.

If I was going to earnestly try to find love in New York, I

decided I would have to get out of my comfort zones. I figured I had three comfort zones that were preventing me from finding love: comedy non-boyfriends, gal pals, and gays. Quick breakdown: Comedy non-boyfriends are the *SNL* guys, good friends like Will Forte or Seth Meyers or writer dudes you absolutely love and they love you too and you can laugh all night in a big group, stay out late, and even flirt, but that's as far as it goes. They serve the purpose of a sparkly and fun boyfriend in your life without the actual relationship or intimacy. I knew them so well that we were like siblings, so anything beyond that would be highly weird, and I'd always opt for the ease and fun of hanging with them rather than going out and trying to meet strangers.

As for gal pals, I had an array of quality ladies to hang with that were funny, wise, and entertaining. Basically, I could go out with a different lady friend every night of the week . . . to a movie, to dinner, for drinks. I could have a really fun time and dish the dirt and be out on the town, but rarely did I meet a guy on one of these evenings.

Gays? See: gal pals. The evening typically had the same outcome.

Imagine my glee when forcing myself out of the comfort zone gave me results: A cute guy who seemed nice and funny asked me out. I had been invited to a holiday party by a friend named Henry, whom I met at Burning Man a few years back. Yes, I, Rachel, went to Burning Man—odd, since I'm not into doing drugs or walking around without my shirt on, which are the two most popular activities that occur at Burning Man.

I went one year with one of my best friends, also named

Rachel, who has gone to Burning Man every summer for eight years. If you aren't familiar with Burning Man, it's a festival out in the middle of a desert in Nevada, where you have to bring in all your own food, supplies, tents, RVs, what have you. Forty thousand people descend on this spot and it becomes an encampment for a week. Like I said, drugs are big there. There are also seminars. The favorite description I saw was for a seminar on oral sex that you were supposed to attend with your partner. It advised, "Bring wipes. The desert can give you that not-so-fresh feeling."

The coolest part about Burning Man to me were the huge art installations, some several stories high, which are truly

amazing. There are also "art cars": Someone will take, say, an old school bus and magically transform it into a light-up dinosaur that, when driven through the desert at night, is absolutely beautiful. That said, one Burning Man was enough for me. I'm not an eight-timer like my friend Rachel. I'm no high-maintenance traveler, but being out in the

A sculpture of a fifty-foot woman in the middle of the desert—just another day at Burning Man.

middle of the desert with inconveniently located port-a-potties when you are *not* high on some drug to make you *think* you are somewhere else just isn't really my jam. You had to trudge to the port-a-potties because, environmentally and hygienically speaking, you just can't have forty thousand people peeing in the middle of the desert, even if there is nothing around for miles for the rest of the year. One night, though, we were out on the Playa, as it's called, the huge miles-long stretch of desert, where everyone's looking at the light-up art installations and art cars and generally checking out the scene. It's completely dark except for people's encampments and the art cars, so you need to carry a flashlight and wear lights on your clothes in order to not get flattened by a moving art vehicle or by a naked person on a bike. I didn't know where the heck I was or where the nearest port-a-potties were located, and I had to pee. So Rachel told me to bend down right there on the Playa. Even though there are people everywhere, you are in almost complete darkness. One of the dangers of peeing in this situation that never crossed my mind was the possibility of an eighty-foot metal robot just happening to shine it's megawatt beam of light down upon me at that moment. But let me warn you now, that can happen at Burning Man. It wasn't the Pee Robot Police. It was just an accidental intersection of art and human need. Flooded in bright white light as if I were in a sci-fi movie, I frantically struggled to pull up my pants, getting pee all over myself in the process. Besides having the social instinct to not be caught with my pants down, for a second I was consumed with the primal fear that this robot was going to fix its metal eye on me, lean in, pick me up, and fling me across the desert.

A lot of people walk around naked at Burning Man, as I said. There's no pressure to be naked—there are plenty of clothed people, myself being one of them. But I expected a sort of hippie vibe about the nudity—grit and grime and drum circles and chicks with hairy armpits. I didn't expect the Sexy Cat Syndrome to be alive and well in the middle of the desert. I can report to you that at Burning Man, Sexy Cat Syndrome is in full effect. By that I mean that there are plenty of women there who would never dress up as a witch or ghost on Halloween. Even though they were San Fran Nature Girls, come Halloween they'd be Sexy Cats as much as any Bridge and Tunnel chick who comes into NYC on the weekends. Or maybe instead they'd say, "I'm a space fairy!" but still find a way to wear just a G-string and some wings. These chicks had supermodel bodies and were traipsing around the desert in nothing but silver Grace Jones boots and body paint. Where were the old ladies with long gray hair and low-hangers? I'd come to the middle of the desert expecting a spiritual experience, only to feel the kind of physical inadequacy usually reserved for seeing a Victoria's Secret ad. Fantastic. Although I saw plenty of these hot chicks with impossibly high boobs and long legs, the men who seemed inclined to disrobe, much fewer in number, were all Haight-Ashbury throwbacks over the age of seventy with long beards and leathery skin. Where was the equity?

Through all the desert madness at Burning Man, I did meet this character Henry. Though he is a Stanford businessman in real life, at the time I met him at our "camp" in Black Rock City, Nevada, he was wearing black nail polish and a man-skirt. He lived near me in New York, which brings me back to my search for love and Henry's Christmas party. The good thing about Henry's party was that Henry isn't an actor. Because he's in business, there would be a whole new crop of people for me to meet. I even turned down my friend Chris when he offered me a free ticket to *Billy Elliot* on the same night, thinking to myself, "No, Rachel! You cannot go to the Broadway musical with your gay friend. You must 'get out there.'" It was a whole new me.

So, on a December evening, I went by myself to Henry's party, where I barely knew anyone. My friend Daisy agreed to meet me there, but she was late, so I was going to have to—*gasp*—talk to strangers. I was over by the bar and food table, as I am wont to be, and right away, as if it were predestined, a man appeared. For the purposes of this story, I'll call him Steve. But his real name was Brent.

"Hi!" I said. There was an odd-looking appetizer on a plate, and I turned to him and boldly continued, "What do you think those are?" It's highly uncharacteristic of me to just say hi to someone I don't know out of the blue, but here I was, chatting up a stranger, a cute, clean-cut, businessman-looking stranger.

At this point, I must interject and say that, in retrospect, I think I had been subconsciously emboldened by a cheesy reality show I had been watching at the time: *The Pickup Artist.* If you've never had the pleasure of seeing this program, the basic premise is this: A guy named Mystery, who is, in actuality, a total tool, teaches über-nerds how to pick up chicks. He wears fur hats and nail polish, and dresses like a wannabe rock star attending a Renaissance Faire. It is reality television at its finest. One of Mystery's main theses is that it doesn't really matter

WHAT you are talking about, just as long as you say anything at all to your potential pickup. So when I asked this man about the strange appetizers, although I'm embarrassed to admit it, I think I was channeling the master himself, Mystery.

We had a bit of chitchat going on and then I asked him his name, unfortunately just as he put some food in his mouth. He chewed while giving me the "just a second" finger in the air, swallowed, and returned with "I know what you do and I'd expect you to have better timing than that." Pretty slick. That was kind of the coolest way anyone has said they recognized me from TV. I ended up talking to him all night long. It was exactly how meeting your boyfriend is supposed to go. I started asking him questions right when he put food in his mouth. Bite. "Whereyoufrom?" Bite. "HowdoyouknowHenry?"

When he told me he grew up in New York City, I said that I had always pictured people who grew up in the city as hard-living kids, doing cocaine on the subways at age fifteen. I realized in hindsight that I was engaging in yet another one of Mystery's techniques: "Negging." Negging is where you throw out a slightly negative comment toward the other person, like "You have bad timing" or "You were probably a coke addict by age fifteen," and for some reason, rather than causing offense, it draws the other person in.

"Steve" and I were totally hitting it off. If you are reading this and thinking, "Big deal, this happens to me every weekend," then I commend you. I must tell you that this kind of thing rarely happened to me. He was supereasy to talk to, and he seemed funny too. And he was a biologist, which in my opinion is a pretty hot profession. To others, maybe a rock star or actor sounds like a hot profession to date, but not to me. Not anymore. Having dated only comedians, I was ready for a nice stable scientist like Steve, who worked for a biotech company. He was successful, funny, well traveled, and fluent in Japanese. At this point, I wasn't hiding my interest. When he told me he was fluent in Japanese, I pretended to swoon and fan myself.

We talked all night and laughed a lot. At one point, we were chatting about our favorite restaurants in the city. When I told him mine, he responded with, "I've never been. We should go there sometime." It was all happening so effortlessly! At the end of the night, he got my number. I felt like this was how things happened in the movies, not in real life.

The next morning, I woke up a little giddy, reliving all the little jokes and laughs and fun flirtiness we had shared. "Hold up, Dratch," warned my inner voice. "You've had these fun flirtations before. And then . . . nothing!" As a matter of fact, at Henry's holiday party the previous year, I had met this cool British accountant who, no joke, had just come back from Africa, where he was building wells for orphans or something. We had talked the night away and even gotten a drink afterward. And then . . . nothing. I never heard from him again. So I was thinking to myself, "Remember the Brit! Don't get ahead of yourself."

Then a magical thing happened—Steve texted me at noon that day. He even asked me out right then for the upcoming weekend. A Friday or Saturday night. Those are the nights normal people go on dates, right? I skipped through the week. Knowing that there was even the potential of love changed my whole demeanor. Then on Thursday, I went to Trader Joe's.

I was at the checkout at Trader Joe's and when I reached down to pick up my bag of groceries, *SPROING!* went my back. The bag wasn't even that heavy. Why was this my luck? Did God not want me to date?

It actually wasn't the first time this back thing had happened. The other time was much worse. It was during a read-through of *SNL*. I had stumbled while walking back to my seat, and my back went out big-time. You know that feeling of a leg cramp? Imagine that in your back but ten times worse and lasting hours. I lay down on the floor and couldn't move an inch. My back was totally spazzing out, and I was writhing in pain. At read-throughs, as I described, the entire staff is there—writers, actors, designers, Lorne, and the host (in this case, Johnny Knoxville). They sent for a doctor, who, upon her arrival, asked if anyone had any pain relievers—muscle relaxants, Vicodin, Percocet—anything. Picture if this had been the original cast from the 1970s. An avalanche of pills would have spilled out onto the table—ludes, pot, speedballs, red bennies, and all those other fun nicknames I learned about in seventh-grade health class. I mean, for God's sake, Johnny Knoxville was the host! I thought surely he would have some heavy pain meds due to his *Jackass* stunts. Well, actually, he did have them, but they were back in his hotel room. There was nothing anyone could do; I just had to wait for the meds to arrive. The read-through continued as I lay under the conference table with someone else reading my parts. Every so often, Lorne would say, "Is Rachel OK down there?" No, I wasn't. I couldn't even respond. I was too busy squeezing the hell out of the doctor's hand. After about two hours, I was able to get up again. I never had a problem since then. Until now. At Trader Joe's.

The only upside was that this time wasn't nearly as bad as the time at *SNL*, but it was the same spot in my back. I walked home like an old lady, shuffling one foot in front of the other. I gingerly tried lying on the floor and stretching, willing the injury to go away. I had my big date on Saturday night (I can't write that sentence without acknowledging it sounds totally like Marcia Brady). This was the first date I was actually excited about in . . . well, probably forever. The few formal dates I'd actually had were always blind dates set up by one of my mother's friends, and, well, you can write that story yourself. People would convince me to go on these dates, against my better judgment. They'd say things like "You never knooooooow! . . . Sometimes these things take tiiiiiime!" I didn't even need convincing this time and here I was, laid out like some old biddy from my mom's aqua-aerobics class.

Friday passed with no improvement. I woke up Saturday morning and it was the same. And I was meeting this guy *tonight*. Basically, I could stand and walk OK, but sitting was hard. That's pretty sexy, right? Anxiety started to creep in, and I began to worry that total back spaz à la *SNL* would happen during my date. I could just imagine myself sprawled out on the floor of some restaurant in the East Village, waiting for an ambulance. I talked to my friends on the phone. "How about acupuncture?" one of them said. Acupuncture. I'd never tried it before.

Ordinarily, I'd be scared of the needles, but at this point I was thinking the needles couldn't be any worse than the pain in my back. I made a few calls to acupuncturists who were recommended, but none were available on such short notice on a Saturday. I was desperate. That's when I turned to the acupuncturist who did NOT come recommended. Here's a tip: Acupuncture is one of those businesses for which I can now attest *Get a reference. Do some research. Make sure they come recommended.*

My friend Chris had gotten massages at one of those Chinese storefront massage/acupuncture places that are quite common in New York. I had even met the doctor of eastern medicine there once when I accompanied Chris. He seemed like a good guy. Chris called the place for me, and they said they could see me right away. The date was six hours away, and I needed a miracle.

I discovered upon arrival that instead of the doctor I had met before, a woman would be performing my treatment. I took one look at her and thought, "Uh-uh." I was quite convinced, and still am, that she was primarily a masseuse whom they let do a bit of acupuncture on the side when the real acupuncturist was off on Saturdays. But in I went, ignoring my gut feeling, following her back to the table. By the way, here's another tip for you: One thing you might not want in a medical establishment is the smell of cat pee.

"I've never done this before. I'm kind of nervous," I said to her.

"DON'T BE NERVOUS!" she commanded in her thick Chinese accent.

Between the language barrier and my sneaking suspicion that this woman was not a legitimate acupuncturist, the appointment unraveled from there. I honestly don't think she even understood why I was there in the first place. I kept trying to tell her that I was there for a specific injury and that my back had pulled out, but she just responded with "OK! YOU WANT SHOULDER TOO?"

I was on the table, facedown and trying to relax, when without warning, she stuck the first needle into the back of my knee. AGHHHHH! It felt like it was hitting a nerve that it wasn't supposed to be hitting. A painful twinge shot up my leg. She went to work with the other needles, sticking them in quick succession into the back of my other knee and the insides of both ankles. I cried out in pain as she continued, sticking needles into my lower back. The ones that went into my lower back weren't as bad. They actually felt the way I was expecting the whole process to feel. But she kept going back to the ones in my knees and repeatedly twisting them. It was so excruciating that at one point, I started shouting, "Not the knee! *Not the knee!*" There were mere curtains separating me from the other clients getting massages. I'm sure they were wondering to themselves, "What is going on behind Curtain Number 4?" I really tried to stay calm, but my mind kept going to thoughts of Josef Mengele. I actively had to steer my brain away from that: *Think of the beach. Think of the beach. Mengele. Beach. Beach. Mengele. Beach. Mengele.*

Finally, it was done. I felt exactly the same. Except now I had to direct my brain away from thinking of the knee needles lest I be overcome with nausea. But after all that, I wasn't giving up. Chris, who is a doctor, came over and shot me up with what he described as "Motrin from outer space." I went out on the date.

I met Steve at the restaurant. My back problem wasn't apparent to the naked eye, but I was in a lot of pain. It's hard to be fully present, let alone witty, charming, and energetic, when you are fighting through pain. We didn't have the same sparkly rapport we had at the party, and a few little red flags went up for me, but I decided to keep them to myself and not tell my friends afterward in case I went out with him again and the red flags turned out to be nothing. But overall I thought it went OK. He told me he was leaving on a two-week business trip the following morning; and after that, I was going to LA for two months to do a play. There was, however, a little window of time we'd overlap back in New York before I left, and we agreed we'd see each other again.

Since I see no harm in it, I'll share the first red flag with you now. An old, familiar, boring red flag: drinking. This guy could really put away the booze. When we moved from the bar (where he had had two drinks) to our table, I still had a nearly full glass of wine. He ordered us a bottle at the table, out of which he probably had four glasses. I'm thinking, "Maybe he's nervous?" Then we continued on post-dinner to a new bar, where he had two more drinks plus one more for us to "share" since it was one of those trendy bars that makes crazy cocktails and he wanted to try absinthe or some shit like that. So his grand tally for the evening was nine drinks. He didn't appear superdrunk, either, except for that sweaty red-faced bleary-eyed glow that can overtake someone who has had nine drinks. Since it was a long date (about six hours) and due to the afore-mentioned "maybe it's nerves," I thought I should still give it another go.

This particular red flag continued to wave in the air, however, when he sent me e-mails from his business trip.

First from London: "Trying to rest my liver today! Not likely to happen with these business parties!"

Then on to Tokyo: "Spending every evening in my friend's whiskey bar!"

Cue downward-note slide whistle: *Woooooooh*. These e-mails did nothing to lower the red flag on the pole in my head. If anything, they were trading it up to a larger size.

Having dated the Three Addicts, I had a whole supply of red flags. Still, I didn't want my potentially hair-trigger red flaggery to keep me from exploring a possibility. So when Steve returned from his business trip and asked me out for that Friday, I agreed. I spent all day in rehearsal for the play, but I still hadn't heard from him at six that evening. I sent him a text: "Are we still on for tonight?"

I received a *text*, not a phone call, but a text that said, "I'm stuck at this work thing. Maybe I can see you when you are back from LA."

Aaaand face plant. What the fahkity freakin' FAHHHHCK? Is this what dating is? He asked me out for a second date just a few days prior, and he didn't even bother to *call* me to tell me he was backing out at the very last second. And he said maybe we could meet up again *two months* from now? Just as our glowy, flirty, first encounter brought to mind scenes from a good romantic comedy, this too felt like something out of a movie. I was being stood up, movie-style!

I was crushed. And not because I thought he was *the one*—I still had those red flags. It was that this guy wasn't a flaky, narcissistic actor. He was a business guy from the real world who spoke several languages and had a real job and asked women out on real dates for Saturday nights and, guess what? He was just as much a flaky narcissist as any actor. So—and I shake my head cartoon-style when I say this—these kinds of guys were everywhere. This guy just happened to be wearing a button-down shirt.

I guess that meant I was now free to tell my friends about the other red flag. I could unfurl it to them and now to the world. We weren't getting married, we weren't even making out. So here goes.

When we were sitting at the second bar, he was telling me about Tokyo. He mentioned that in Tokyo there are restaurants that serve only horsemeat.

"Euggghhh!" I said, making a face.

"No," said he, "it's the most delicious meat you will ever eat in your life."

"I don't knoooww," said I.

"Deeee-licious," said he, marveling in it a bit too much.

Maybe I was being culturally biased. I'm not a vegetarian, so what's the difference between a horse and a cow? I guess. But horses are noble beasts! Are you supposed to tell a woman you adore the taste of horsemeat on a first date? There was something a bit off about the way he was reveling in it. I could see some of the *SNL* dudes telling the same story, but there would be a dose of humor in the delivery. Instead, I got a creepy vibe. Besides, what if I had been one of those horsey girls as a child, with plastic statuettes and blue ribbons on my wall? Lucky for him, I wasn't, but isn't telling a girl you just loooooove eating horsemeat one step away from saying you haven't lived 'til you've eaten puppy skewers?

Then he said, "Have you ever wondered what it would be like to taste human flesh?"

I'll let that sit for a second.

"No," I said.

"Really? Come on, you've never even wondered what it would be like? Would you try it if you were given the opportunity?"

"No!" I exclaimed. There wasn't anything cute and funny about his tone as if he were posing the question in a humorous parlor game. Rather, it seemed like he had given this topic some thought.

"Why not?" said he.

"Because I would just be wondering *who* is this person and *how* did they end up on my plate. Would you?"

His response to this question made the phrase "Silence of the Lambs" pop into my head. He told me unequivocally that yes, he definitely was curious and would taste human flesh if given the chance. But it was almost like he was actively seeking out this opportunity. Like maybe, somewhere in his world travels, he'd be lucky enough to discover a restaurant called Cannibals! *Try Our Breaded Human Fingers!*

He continued, saying something about how when he would cauterize pigs in the science lab (don't ask . . . I never did), the smell of bacon would fill the air and it would make him crave bacon. I think the implication was that when he did procedures or experiments on human cadavers, it made him hungry. I guess I'd have to add "Scientist (Mad)" to my list of Do Not Date professions.

I never saw or heard from Steve again. In hindsight, getting blown off via text was probably a blessing in disguise. And maybe the fact that my back went out was actually a gift. Maybe it's not that God didn't want me to date, but rather that God was actually sifting out the bad stuff for me through a divine intervention at Trader Joe's. I may have narrowly avoided spending the rest of my nights with a man who drinks whole bottles of wine at a table for two, sharing the braised human abs or the triceps risotto.

Body by Shtetl

The experience with Brent—oh, sorry, *Steve*— definitely put a dent in my morale. He seemed like such a nice guy at the party. In reality, he was just a douche in sheep's clothing.

The worst thing about this was now I was going to have to "get out there" again, and in terms of "getting out there" I've never exactly been one to strut my stuff. When I was in my twenties, I had terrible posture; I was always hunched over, trying to hide my huge jugs. All of my ancestors on both sides of the family come from the same general region, what was then the Jewish area of what is now the Ukraine. That means basically that I am of 100 percent Russian/Ukrainian Jewish peasant stock. You could drop me into any production of *Fiddler on the Roof*, throw a kerchief on my head, and I'd fit right in. (You hear that, Hollywood?! . . . What's that, Hollywood? . . . Nooo, I don't think there were any lesbians in *Fiddler on the Roof*. Though now that I think of it, Yente the Matchmaker may have tendencies—Oh, forget it, Hollywood!) The point is my body is 100 percent shtetl. This is especially apparent in

The seven Pick sisters (Great-Grandma Sarah is in the top row, second from the left.)

my ankles, which are basically nonexistent, and in my huge jugs. I mention this because recently I found a picture of my great-grandmother and her six sisters posing for an Old Country Photo Shoot. I took one look at it and burst out laughing. Each sister in the photo has total shtetl bod, many with their own set of genuine, nature-made Torpedo Tits. No *wonder* I had these boobs; they were of my *people.* but I was still fighting them in my head.

Back in my twenties, I caught a glimpse of myself on tape at Second City, saw how horrible my posture was, and decided "That's it! I'm going to stand up straight!" This really happened: About an HOUR after I had that conscious thought, I was walking down Belmont Street in Chicago. I think I was wearing a white T-shirt, and a guy who was dressed like a seventies pimp, complete with one of those puffy patchwork hats and skinny bell-bottom pants, said to me in a low and slow and creepy voice as he walked by: "Big Tiiiits."

Blech.

As gross as that was, I wasn't going to let it deter my posture mission. However, the *very next day* as I was entering the theater, and standing up straight, some guys yelled out of a car, "Nice tits!" Was I in some movie where a character makes a decision, and reactions happen to them *this* fast? I don't mean good reactions—I mean *this* is why it's better to hide what you're packin' unless you are Ice-T's wife, Coco, and you want to make a living off of that attention.

The only time I know for sure that I was the object of someone's illicit fantasies was in a dark movie theater—the Music Box in Chicago. A man entered the theater when the movie was almost over and sat down a few seats away. I had the feeling he was looking at me and then I saw that his hand was going at it. I abruptly hissed to my friend, "That man is masturbating!" and moved my seat quickly. I was pissed because this was the end of the movie, and I wanted to pay attention, and I didn't have time for this nonsense. This is a pretty run-of-the-mill man-masturbating-in-a-movie-theater story, I know, but what I find unique about my tale is I was watching *Europa Europa*. I had a man whack off to me during the last ten minutes of a Holocaust movie.

No, I could hardly characterize myself as lucky in love. I'm even the only person I know who managed to get a sexually transmitted disease by having no sexual contact whatsoever. One summer when I was living in Chicago, I went to a cottage with a friend of mine named Alice. Her family had rented the cottage along Lake Michigan up in some little resort town. We spent the weekend there—myself, her dad, some of her siblings. She comes from a huge family. Partway through the day on Sunday, I began to feel some itching in my nether regions. Anyway, I got back home to Chicago and I was on the phone with a friend—not a really good friend, more an outer-circle friend. There was that itching again. While I was on the phone, I took a peek down south and I noticed that there were some little dots on my skin. Yes, I'm still on the phone while this is happening. I pick at one of the little dots and, upon closer examination, I look at it and discover that IT IS MOVING.

BLAAAACGHHH. HEAVE. HURL. I can't tell this particular person on the phone what is happening, so I am in a gagging panic while trying to carry on a conversation, all the while realizing that somehow, without having had any sex . . . I got crabs. Welp, if that was going to happen to anyone, I'd vote me.

These were the days before the Internet, so I couldn't look up what to do. I had to wait it out, through that long and crabby night, until morning, when I could call my doctor, who said, "Now, you're sure you didn't have sexual contact with anyone?" Yeah, I'm sure. I mean, does this ever happen to anyone? "Well, I suppose it *could*." I was a damn medical miracle.

The cottage where we had spent the weekend was quite rustic and it was a rental and who knew what was lurking in those mattresses? Well, I knew. That's actually who knew. Alice's family was staying there the whole week, and I figured, in spite of the embarrassing nature of my news and in spite of the fact that I didn't know Alice's family all that well, I should tell them, nay, *warn* them as a sort of "Do unto others" Golden Rule of Pubic Lice. I felt obliged to let them know their whole family was in grave danger of bringing home a tribe of six-legged beasts in their genitals. So I told Alice.

In a highly unsatisfying response, rather than being thanked for my honesty and candor, I ended up being somewhat shamed. She got back to me the next day, saying something oddly vague, like, "Yeah, no one's had any problems!" in a bright and casual voice. Nothing like, "We thoroughly washed the towels, the sheets; we doused the mattresses with buckets of boiling alcohol; we made a stern phone call to inform the people we were renting from . . ."—all of the emergency measures I expected to hear about. I could practically hear them sitting around the dinner table. "That dirty slut girl and her crabs! And she's trying to pass them off on our salt-of-the-earth Midwest wholesome family. Ha-haaaa! Who wants another sloppy joe?!"

Alice's implication seemed to be that I must have gotten them somewhere else, maybe while I was out ho'ing around, for all her family knew. No, I hadn't been out ho'ing around—I just had the unique luck of managing to get an STD without any S.

Dating the Fonz

After Horsemeat, I was still determined to try, try again. I would have to redouble my efforts and turn my Dick-head Filters to their highest settings. You see, I was looking for a *Nice Guy.*

I had always had a problem with Nice Guys in the past. I didn't know it at the time, but it was *my* problem. Well, Nice Guys, hear ye, hear ye: I paid for it dearly. I think it all started in eighth grade. It may be a common teenage girl trait to go for a real asshole. Did I watch too much *Happy Days* as a child? I did have socks with Fonzie on them in fourth grade that were my pride and joy. Did I learn everything about boys from a guy who snaps his fingers and several nameless girls come running to him, not minding that they aren't the only one and will have the light of the Fonz shining on them only for mere moments? Somewhere in my brain, "nice" did not equal boyfriend material. What was sexy about nice?

In eighth grade, I had my first encounter with a nice boy who liked me. Chris was a gem. To ask me out, he sent me a singing telegram through some service that would call you up and sing the "telegram" to you on the phone. I still remember the words.

Excuse me if I'm shy
But on you I've had my eye
Please accept a date with me
At least give it a try
You know it would be great
If you'd accept this date
Please say yes and I'll be happy
If you will be my date!

I was flattered, I was tickled. I genuinely *liked* this guy. I called him up and said yes. I think that was the first boy who ever asked me out. Well, except for this guy named Matt in seventh grade. We "dated" for one week until he broke up because I was "spending too much time with my friends." The funny thing about Matt was, he left our town soon after eighth grade, but when I was at Dartmouth, I saw his name in the class below mine. I asked him—"Are you Matt who used to live in Lexington?" He said yes, but he had absolutely no recollection of me and didn't seem at all amused by my attempt at junior high nostalgia. I think he gave me a blank stare and a grunt. Throw that onto the Dartmouth pile.

But as for Chris, the first Nice Guy, the Nicest of the Nice—after the singing telegram, I think we were kind of seeing each other, although we had no physical contact whatsoever. This was a simpler time. Or I was just a simple girl. Once we were at a "boy/girl party"—that's what we called them back then; these days they are probably called "blow-job parties"—and he asked me if I wanted to "take a walk." Code for making out. I said no! I knew nothing of making out. I think I was just scared. I didn't want to. And besides, he was nothing like Fonzie. Where was his swagger, his underlying adolescent boy assholery? It wasn't there. He played the trombone. He would go on to Haverford.

I know we went on one date. Again, I was terrified. I didn't know how to be alone with a boy. So what did I do? I *brought a friend.* To the naked eye, I was just being an annoying junior high school girl, but again I was driven by fear. Chris' dad picked us up and drove me and my friend and him to the Burlington Mall. I think I bought a Wiffle ball.

Cut to, now we are juniors in high school, long after our awkward junior high breakup, which consisted of me coming back from the summer and saying I thought we should break up (even though all we ever did to "date" was chat on the phone) and then ignoring him because of my own massive awkwardness. I was in a play, and after the show, Chris gave me flowers with a note that said "*From your not-so-secret admirer.*" The Nicest of the Nice was back.

We didn't run in the same crowds, per se. We were both in the smart classes, but like I said, I hung out with more the jock/party-in-the-woods crew. (Fun Fact: Many of them are named in the "Sully and Denise" sketch we did on *SNL* with Ben Affleck.) I bumped into Chris in the hallway soon after the flowers incident, and he asked me out on a date. By now we were sixteen or seventeen, but I may as well have been thirteen with my level of comfort in dating. Then came the moment in my life I wish I could take back. I'm sure there's more than one, but I think this one haunts me because I was young. It's the sort of moment from your youth that you wish you could go back with your adult brain and fix for yourself and, more importantly, for the injured party.

Lest you get the wrong picture, Chris wasn't only Nice. He wasn't some milquetoast character from the movies. He was really smart, and he was funny too, and he was a cute guy. He called me up to set up our date. By now, my thirteen-year-old fear brain had taken over and I wasn't looking forward to the date. I really don't know why. Because he showed such fervent interest in me? Because I needed that danger or swagger in him or a feeling of inferiority in myself to feel interested? When he called to set the date up, though, he was turning on the charm. He had given a lot of thought to this and he sug-gested dinner and a movie—dinner at Bel Canto, one of the Italian restaurants in town. This was the classier joint with white cloth tablecloths, a step above Mario's, which had vinyl red-checkered tablecloths. I remember he said that we could get a romantic table in the corner or something like that, a concept that sent me mentally fleeing. In the middle of this call, the other phone line rang. I was on my parents' phone with Chris and said, "Could you hold on a sec?" and picked up the "kids' line"—the ancient equivalent of call-waiting. It was my friend Eve. "Eve! I don't know what to do! Chris is on the other line and he's talking about this date. He's making it all romantic and stuff. What should I do? Now I don't want to go!" I don't quite remember the words but it was something along those lines. "He's talking about a romantic table in the corner! Oh my God!"

I flipped back to Chris to continue begrudgingly making these plans. "Hi. I'm back."

"Hi. You know, you can hear through to the other line on this phone."

"Huh? . . . Oh."

My mind didn't comprehend that this could be true. What was he talking about? Was that really possible? In a slight panic, I went forward, not addressing what he had just said at all. Here's where I wish I had some adult judgment working for me and had actually addressed what had happened.

I awkwardly hurried off the phone with Chris. I discovered in the next few days after running some tests that indeed, through a glitch in the phone system, you could hear the other line. I didn't mention it to Chris, apologize, explain, attempt to make an excuse, anything. I simply ignored it. We did go out to a movie and it was hurried and perfunctory. By then I was in full dread mode, only compounded by my gaffe. We went to see *Airplane 2* and didn't go out to dinner before or after. I was treating it like an unpleasant appointment I had made and just had to get through.

Class act that he was, he never held my immaturity or rudeness, depending on how you want to frame it, against me. Our senior year, he signed my yearbook. I was with my friends after school, hanging out on the benches, when I sat down to read what he wrote. It was the first time I can remember crying not out of sadness but from sweetness. This is what he wrote:

"Rachel—There was a time when I would have done any-thing for you, and I mean anything. I wanted to be, and I guess I still do, your Errol Flynn, Cary Grant, and Indiana Jones all rolled up into one. You are a truly beautiful person. You will wow 'em wherever you go. Remember that scene from *Raiders of the Lost Ark* where he lassos the girl and pulls her in to him? Well . . . that's what I'd like to do with you."

I *know.* I was a damn idiot.

Scarce few men have said anything that sweet or poi-gnant to me since then. Chris appears to me regularly in dreams where I am trying to right my own wrong, not just to him but to myself, I imagine, for not accepting that kind of sweetness and love. In my dreams I always say to him, "Oh my gosh! I have dreams about you!" He never says anything back. Do I have to keep having this dream until, within the dream, he responds? After years and years of these dream appear-ances, I Googled him and discovered through my rudimentary detective work that he married his college sweetheart and is a lawyer with two kids who at some point lived in New York City and, I think, even converted to Judaism—you can learn quite a bit from Google.

I passed up many nice guys after Chris too, opting instead to fling myself into a world of charismatic guys to be "won over," a world of Fonzies. "Aaaaay!" Guess what I learned. Dat-ing Fonzie sucks. I was ready to find myself a Richie Cunning-ham. I'd even settle for a Ralph Malph.

Unfortunately for me, it took years to learn this lesson. I

was off on my unconventional career path, which meant I was surrounded by people for whom staying out 'til four in the morning on a Wednesday night was perfectly normal and acceptable, if that's what you felt like doing. While everyone else, like my friends from home and college, was finding love, partnering off, and starting families, I dated the Three Addicts. I was never so into substances myself, ever since I had eaten a "space cake" in Amsterdam at age twenty and thought I was going to die. I at once took a solemn vow to never ingest another drug that can't be undone—i.e., 'shrooms, coke, ecstasy, black tar heroin . . . never touched the stuff. I like the fact that when you are demurely sipping a glass of red wine, you aren't going to suddenly take one sip that makes you think the tiles on the floor are moving.

With no history of addiction in my family, I don't know how I managed to ferret these gentlemen out, but ferret I did! I dated the alcoholic (since recovered, dear friend), the pot-head (a stand-up comic—an even worse choice of boyfriend than an improviser. When you think about it, an improviser has to relate to people and be part of a group mind, while a stand-up just has to be willing to travel to Florida by himself and stay at a Days Inn), and finally, because I'm a comedian and adhere to the Rule of Threes, I rounded it all out with a sex addict. (Rule of Threes: If you do something two times in a scene, you have to do it a third time to get the laugh.) I didn't even know this guy was a sex addict while we were dating. And I had my antennae out too! He didn't drink or do drugs—a virtual teetotaler! But I found out later I had done it again and found another addict. Rule of Threes! By the time I had finally learned my lesson, I was thirty-eight years old.

SNL had always served as a handy excuse to myself for why I didn't have a boyfriend. "I'm too busy!" I'd tell myself. During the workweeks, we were indeed too busy to have much of an outside social life, but the fact is that we did have plenty of weeks off during the year, plus the entire summer. No matter, I could always rely on the old phrase "It will happen when you're not looking!" That's what people would always tell me anyway. These people are NEVER single, by the way. Have you ever, ever had a friend who is single say to you, "It will happen when you're not looking"? No. You haven't. The people that say it always have a bright smile, happily ensconced in a relationship. *"It will happen when you're not looking!"*

Well, I could "not look" like a champ! Not looking is easy! You just do whatever you want to do, whenever you want to do it. Of course, this strategy completely goes against the other 50 percent of the time when *those same people* tell you, "Get out there! Don't sit at home!" or "My cousin went on Match.com and now she's *married*!"

I personally went in waves, between shut down/not looking and getting out there. Then, when I could no longer stand "getting out there" another minute, another night at a bar I didn't want to be drinking in, another party on a night I felt like staying home and watching TV, another evening with my not-usual crowd, I would duck back into the comfort zone for a while. Then the comfort zone would start to scare me and I'd hurl myself back "out there" again. Until someone again told me, "It'll happen when you're not looking!" Oh, they'll keep saying it. The only more incomprehensible statement I can think of is when people say, "Well, he died doing what he loved," and they take comfort in that. "Did you hear? Joe was killed in a hang-gliding accident." "Well, he died doing what he loved!" I'm sure Joe would rather have lived while cleaning his toilet than die hang gliding.

But now here I was—post-Addicts, post-*SNL*, post-*30 Rock*, post-any-employment-whatsoever. I had no excuses. I was ready to tackle dating with the hard-earned maturity of an adult and, feeling I was trying to start fresh, with the wide-eyed naïveté of a sixteen-going-on-seventeen-year-old dancing around the gazebo, without the teenaged boobs to match. At the same time, and Horsemeat didn't help, I had the bitter, seen-it-all cynicism of a WWII vet: Something in me was pretty sure that by the time I was this age, my early forties, all the Nice Guys who wanted a real relationship had already married their college sweethearts and converted to Judaism.

"She's Siiiinngle!"

One night in the midst of this determined state, I was a featured guest on a live talk show that took place in a theater. It was similar to a live Conan or Letterman—a funny host and an audience, but not televised, just a theater piece. During the interview, the host asked me if I was dating anyone special. I said no, I wasn't. He turned to the audience and yelled, "You hear that everyone? She's siiiinngle!"

The interview ended and I walked back to my spot in the audience to rejoin my friend Ryan at our seats in this small theater. No sooner did I sit down, having just been announced as a single lady, than a gentleman appeared next to me in the darkness. The show was still going on and he leaned over and whispered, "Can I get you a drink?"

"No, thanks," I said, ever oblivious to an opportunity.

"Are you sure?"

"Yes, but thank you."

He walked away toward the bar, and Ryan turned and hit my arm. "Hey, he's cute!"

Huh? Is he? I thought about it for a moment. I guess so. I don't know. Not really my type. My type, however, had not worked out for me in the past and should probably have been manually shifted out of its stuck position in my brain. Maybe it was time to go against my type. This guy was your standard NYC Jewish-looking dude that I never went for. He sported a goatee and a newsie cap.

And all of a sudden, he reappeared.

"Here. I got you a water."

"Oh, thanks."

This guy was persistent. I said I didn't want a drink, but I think he must have been, dare I say, hitting on me? I mean, the host had *just* said I was single not five minutes before. He started talking to me, quietly, as the show was still going on. He told me he was a writer for *Gotham* magazine. As the show was ending, he said, "Well, I'm gonna take off now, but here's my card. Call me. We'll go have some fun." Those were his words. "Call me. We'll go have some fun."

This was proof that I just needed to get out of my usual routine! Change it up a little bit. Meet new people. Get out there. Ryan was way into this guy for me, telling me that I *had* to e-mail him.

The next day, Ryan kept pestering me. "OK, did you contact the guy? Did you?"

"No. Not yet."

Ryan is one of my inner-circle gays. We first met at my audition for *SNL*. He worked in the talent office, booking the musical guests. He's of Japanese descent, Mormon-raised though not practicing, Hawaii-born. Remember I said that I lucked out because, for my audition, some people from the office had gathered in the back, so I had people to laugh at my audition instead of a silent void? Ryan was one of those people, and his laugh is loud. Ryan can be so loud, in fact, that sometimes when we are out in public, I have to remind him to use his "restaurant voice."

Our friendship grew at *SNL* because during the time between the read-through and the "picks," that painful three hours when you are operating on no sleep and waiting to see if you will be in the show that week, Ryan would have access to a supply of wine reserved for the talent or perhaps even for Lorne himself—I never knew. But I was a willing participant in its consumption with Ryan on Wednesday nights. It's hard for me to believe it, but Ryan and I overlapped at *SNL* for only one year. Our friendship grew from there, notably on one day in particular. Ryan moved to LA and was visiting in NYC. We had dinner with a group of friends near my apartment on the Upper West Side. Ryan was supposed to stay with a friend in Brooklyn, but the friend was sick and so Ryan asked if he could crash on my couch. We were really just "work friends" at this point. We didn't hang out much on our own. I said sure and he stayed on my couch. The next morning when we woke up, it was 9/11. His mom called him up early and we spent the day watching TV together, seeing the towers collapse there on live TV. Ryan brought the only second of levity to the horrible day when he went to the grocery store to get some supplies. He returned forty-five minutes later, hands flying in an exaggerated gay thing he puts on for laughs, and screamed, "They are *hoarding* at the grocery store!"

In general, our relationship can best be summed up in the following exchange:

The time: eight A.M. My phone rings. "Hello?" I say in a groggy voice.

"Heeeyyyyy!"

"What's going on?"

"I got the best blow job last night."

"IT'S TOO EARLY FOR THIS!" I snap, and hang up on him.

Ryan was one of my many friends who had heard me lament my man situation over the years, and so he was rooting for me on the Dating Crusade. He wouldn't let up about this guy from the theater.

For me, my natural anti-dating instincts started to kick in. I hate dating. I hate strangers. I hate going on dates with strangers. I waited about two weeks until I had managed to work up the will to e-mail him. I went to get his card out of my purse and it wasn't there. I had put it right in the small pocket! I turned the bag over, dumped everything out, and still nothing. It was definitely gone.

I reported back to Ryan that I had lost the card, and he was very disappointed in me. He suggested that we look him up at *Gotham*. We tried, but he wasn't listed. I thought he had mentioned he only freelanced there. Also, the difficulty in locating him was compounded by the fact that he had a pretty common name, so Googling him didn't help. So that was it. I screwed up.

Almost a year later, on my birthday, I was walking down the street in my neighborhood and a guy was walking toward me on the sidewalk, grinning. I didn't even remember him at first; he had to tell me that he was the guy who had talked to me at that show.

"Oh my God! I lost your card!" I exclaimed to him. "I was gonna get in contact with you and I lost it!"

"Well, here's another one," he said and presented a new card. I waited about a week to e-mail him to say hi, due to my aforementioned reluctance and fear. But he immediately wrote me back suggesting we go out to drinks. He even offered four or five venue options. He was very thoughtful and concerned about planning the date at just the right place.

The night of the date, I met him at the bar area of a large Spanish restaurant. There was no instant attraction on my part, but I was trying like hell to be a "regular person" who could get to know somebody slowly. We chatted about this and that, and about ten minutes in, I asked him about his job. He told me about being a freelance writer. He then said, "And my partner and I have a dog-walking business." His . . . business partner, you ask? Nope! His *gay husband partner.* The guy is wearing a ring. He is married to a man. And I was on a date with him.

Now this story goes off in two branches. One branch is, I was pissed. This guy seemed straight to me, and I think of myself as having pretty finely tuned gaydar. He even fooled Ryan. Also, he had approached me *right* after that host announced to the audience, "She's siiiinngle!" and asked me out. I guess this was the drawback of being in the public eye. This guy just wanted to meet someone who was on TV so he could say, "Hey, I'm hanging out with that girl from *SNL* tonight." What other explanation was there? And why would I go out with a complete, gay stranger on a friend date? I have friends, not to mention my full posse of quality gay men friends whom I've met via legitimate means!

Here comes the other branch of the story, and this is why I said nothing to this guy on the "date" but hung in there for an hour before bolting from the area in defeat. Before I was in the public eye, which wasn't until my early thirties, I had a great memory for people I met. I was never someone who forgot a name or a face. But an odd thing happens when you are on TV. People are used to seeing you night after night on their television. You are in their home. They've had a ton of practice at seeing your face. But the reverse isn't true. Sometimes it happens that when I've met a stranger, they'll see me again two years later and think I'm going to remember them from a ten-second introduction at a party, maybe because they've had years of seeing me on TV. After I saw this guy on the street and he gave me his card again, I was walking to the gym one morning a few days later, and a complete stranger passed me and said hello. In my head I was thinking, "Who the hell is this?" That's another thing about being in the public eye; sometimes a person saying hi is just a stranger who recognizes you and is superfriendly. Other times, it's a classmate of yours from high school. Usually, when a stranger says hi as if we are old buddies, my mind goes into superfast Rolodex mode and tries to sort out who the friendly person is. When this guy said hi, I came up blank.

"Hi," I said, Rolodex spinning madly.

"This is my partner, Walt."

"Hi," I say to Walt, an extremely gay man.

"OK. Bye!"

Who was that? "It sort of looked like that guy who had asked me out," went a fleeting thought in my mind that flitted immediately out again. I should have paid attention to that fleeting thought, because I discovered on the date that the gay man who had said hi a few days before on the street was indeed the same man with whom I was currently drinking sangria. So you see, by the time I went out with this guy, I *did* "know" my date was gay. I even met his partner! I had no recourse. I couldn't say, "Why the hell did you ask me out, gay man!?" Because technically, *right* before this date, I had seen him on the street with his partner. I had some severe face blindness syndrome with this guy who, I still contend, looked like the quintessential New York Jewish dude.

This dating thing was doing nothing to improve my morale. I am no "star" in my own mind, yet allow me to use this word for the sake of argument. The only thing worse than going on a date with a starf****r is going on a date with a gay starf****r. With a gay starf****r, you can pretty much be sure there will be no f***ing.

My Pal, the Universe

Clearly, love was not happening. My career still wasn't happening either. I did not want to fall into a k-hole about my life. I was determined to remain positive. I had learned my lesson after I ended my four-year stint on the mainstage at Second City in Chicago and moved to LA, where *nothing* happened in my career for the longest time. I felt really defeated about it. But after a year in LA, I landed the job on *SNL*. I was going to be wiser now. I wasn't going to waste my precious time bumming out, because you never know when your break is coming. However, it was getting harder and harder to stay optimistic. So, next, I did what people do in dark times—I turned to religion. Well, I turned to spirituality. Well, I turned to . . . The Secret.

As in *THE SECRET!* As in that DVD and book that came out several years ago that temporarily made me feel I was invincible and the only thing holding me back from my own success was my own negative attitude. The Secret says that if you envision the life you want and live as if you already have all the good things you desire, the UNIVERSE will magically send all those good things to you. Have you ever tried The Secret? I know that believing in The Secret comes with some shame, but I am sure some of you ladies reading this have a vision board with pictures of engagement rings and babies, and a picture of Oprah so you can someday meet her, and it's stuck behind your dresser in case a guy were ever to come over, see it, and run screaming in terror from your bedroom.

I can tell you from my experience with The Secret that there are two phases. The first is Secret Euphoria. You are the master of your own destiny and can bring whatever you want into your life. You place your order with the Universe, and the Universe delivers everything back that you've requested in a neat bow and in a timely fashion. You try it a bit and you know what? It kind of works. Well, at least it did for me. I had first encountered The Secret a few years prior, and to try it out, I decided I wanted a part in a movie and I wrote it down. The Secret says to aim as high as you possibly can, so I decided to up the ante—a role in a movie *in a cool foreign land*. Yes. I actually wrote it down.

No joke, six months later, I was headed off to Spain and Greece to shoot a comedy with Nia Vardalos. The amazing thing about me getting my wish was that it's very rare for comedies to shoot in amazing foreign locales. Big dramas or war movies, yes, but comedies can usually be shot right at home. So I did think maybe there was something to this Secret thing.

But as anyone who has done The Secret knows, Secret Euphoria is followed by another phase, which I refer to as Secret Crashout. This is the phase when you look at your list and you look at your life and you realize you still don't have a boyfriend or a million dollars or an organized apartment. It's the "Let me get this straight, Universe, you're telling me I DON'T have magical powers?" phase. Hence the term *Secret Crashout.*

I needed a reboot. I needed to get back on track. I just needed to believe again. Well, the DVD says to start small by asking the Universe for something simple, to prove you've got your mojo. It suggests a cup of coffee. In Secretland, that means you envision yourself getting a cup of coffee, a free cup of coffee that just happens into your life merely because you focused on the positive vision in your mind and therefore start vibrating on the frequency that attracts this free cup of coffee. I didn't want to ask for the cup of coffee. That felt too unoriginal, since it's the example they use in the DVD. What could I ask for that could give me a sign? How about a flower? That's simple. I asked for a flower.

Two short days later, I am performing the works of Spalding Gray, *Stories Left to Tell*, as a guest (they had a guest actor sit in every week). I didn't have any friends coming until later in the week, but when I arrived in the dressing room, there on my table was not merely one single flower but three bouquets of gorgeous flowers arranged on the dressing table for me. I looked at my bounty of flowers and gave a sly singsongy wink to the heavens. "Universe! You sly devil!" I thought. Mind you, these flowers were from members of the cast I barely even knew. It was way above and beyond the call of thespian courtesy that there would be flowers from mere acquaintances raining down upon me.

I asked for *a* flower and I got a whole bunch of flowers in return. Yup, everything was going my way. The Universe was back! Back to being my own magical genie.

When I got home, I started to arrange my new flowers. The bottoms of the stems were bound with rubber bands. This is standard NYC-deli flower practice. I got some scissors and cut the first rubber band. *SNAP!* The rubber band flung off the stem quicker than the blink of an eye. I can tell you with great certainty that it happened literally quicker than the blink of an eye because before I could blink my eye, that rubber band had smacked my eyeball like a slingshot. *OWW! Aghh! Owwww!*

The irony occurred to me instantly. While still smarting and futilely rubbing my eye, I was thinking in my you-merry-prankster tone, "U-niverse! Why are you doing this to me? All I wanted was a flower and you gave me a whole bunch of flowers. Why you gotta go and wreck it, Universe?"

The next morning, I woke up and, to my surprise, my eye still really hurt. Now I had to go to the eye doctor. There goes my whole afternoon. Just because I asked for that damn flower. The eye doctor told me that it was a good thing I came in, because I had a severe irritation on my eye. He actually had to prescribe me some drops.

"You'd be surprised how often we see this injury in New York," he told me.

The deli-flowers-rubber-band-eye-snap thing. Beware.

I was walking home from the subway, having spent my entire afternoon tending to my odd karmic injury. I'd better start over again, I thought to myself. Clean slate. I wondered what else I could ask for to get back on The Secret train.

I popped into the Starbucks on my corner and ordered a nonfat latte. As I went to the counter to retrieve my order, the Starbucks employee (no, I am not going to use the word *barista*) handed me my coffee.

"Hey!" he told me. "When I saw you come in, I made you an iced latte 'cause that's what you usually get. So I already made you an iced latte too. Do you want it? We're just gonna throw it away."

Ta-da! The cup of coffee! THE CUP OF COFFEE! From the DVD! After all of my magical thinking, here it was, the thing right from the video that was somehow supposed to represent all of the abundance of life. I walked down the block with my prescription eyedrops in my purse and two coffees in hand and looked skyward. *"U-niveeeeerrrse!!"*

I Left My Heart
(and Dignity) in Sacramento

Before I started my mini-dating tear, it had been three years since I had been in a relationship. That relationship ended in Sacramento.

My fourth summer of *SNL*, I was offered a role in an indie movie, to play the "best friend" role. This was my only foray into the best-friend role because this was a low-budget indie movie, not a big studio venture. In this movie, the leading lady was going to be Estella Warren, the really hot chick from the *Planet of the Apes* remake from 2001.

I was to play her lesbian roommate.

"OK," I said to my agent, "I think I should do this, but I do have one question."

"What's that?"

"In what universe would Estella Warren and I be best friends?"

By this I only meant that I am about fifteen years older

than her, and let's face it, when you put us side by side, you don't really think, "Ah, two peas in a pod! There's ham 'n' cheese! Peanut butter and jelly! And Dratch 'n' Warren!" But this was my chance to play more than a secretary who pops in for a few laughs and is not seen for the rest of the movie. . . . This could bump me up to that coveted "wacky friend" status!

I arrived for the shoot, which for my part would take two weeks, in Sacramento.

I'm sure there are lovely parts of Sacramento. I was exposed only to the Hyatt Hotel and its two-block radius. From this viewpoint, Sacramento is the most white-bread town in the country.

Something went wrong on this movie shoot, in either my life or the shoot itself, or both at the same time, pretty much every day.

Let's start with this: Probably the second day of shooting, I was in my trailer bathroom peeing. I heard a knock on the outside of the trailer door. I feebly tried to shout that I was in the bathroom, but there was no way someone would hear that through two doors. The knock happened again. I ignored it. Next thing I knew, as I was standing up from the toilet, the door swung open to reveal the college kid production assistant who was there to empty a trash can or something. I screamed. This kid had opened the door at the peak moment of full bush exposure. This is the kid who, the day before, had driven me back to the hotel, a drive wherein you make chitchat like "So, where ya from?" and now he had seen me rising from a toilet with my pants at my knees. "Sorry," he blurted out, and bolted from the scene. (I realize this is the second frontal-exposure tale I have shared thus far. In spite of the Rule of Threes, I promise it is the last.) I was surprisingly annoyed. So know that for the rest of the shoot, I was skulking around, trying to avoid this particular kid. Was I cool about it? No, I was not. When I saw him later, did I have a good chuckle about the fact that he had just seen m'bush? No siree. I chose avoidance. This entailed my peering around, like Harriet the Spy, over at the lunch tables when it was time to eat. I was a refugee on my own set in Sacramento.

The director of this movie was Charlie Matthau, son of the late Walter Matthau. Charlie was very friendly, earnest, a bit of a goofball, and he looked just like a young lanky version of his dad.

When I was shooting this film, I was in a relationship with Addict #3 and it was severely on the rocks. I was in complete denial about this relationship. It had probably been over about three months in, though by now we had been together for around a year. But all his "I need my alone time" and "I'm just a guy who likes space" and "Work is the most important thing to me" were not taken as clues by me that this relationship would in no way be a self-esteem builder. So one night during this shoot, I was on the phone with this gentleman and I was getting the picture that I was barely going to see him for the rest of the summer and this did not seem to affect him very much. He was throwing all sorts of trips, jobs, and travels my way, of which I was no part. As the conversation progressed, I was seeing that this thing weren't goin' nowhere. We basically broke up right there on the phone. I was devastated. Really? This was happening on the phone? In Sacramento?

The next morning, I reported to the set in a sea of self-pity and depression. I must say, though, you would not know it to look at me. I didn't know anyone on this set, and I wasn't about to pour out the situation to a stranger. So there we were, on the set of this café (I was a coffeeshop owner instead of a secretary!), about to shoot the scene. Suddenly, a wail rose up from I don't know where. A mournful, keening, horrid cry. I looked around. It was Estella Warren. Out of nowhere, she had broken down into a heap of tears. Granted, this is how I was feeling on the inside, and here it was, all my emotions pouring out of the very full-lipped, *Maxim* mouth of Estella Warren. You see, when I was in the makeup chair that morning, she had casually mentioned that she had failed to connect on the phone with her boyfriend, who lived in LA, at the appointed time the night before. She was talking about it pretty lightheartedly in the makeup chair, like it wasn't a huge deal. I don't know what happened between then and now, an hour later. Maybe the ramifications of the lovers' spat were hitting her hard. Who knows—maybe there was more going on than just the phone call. I'm really not trying to bust on her, the peanut butter to my jelly, but I was thinking about *my* situation and that I REALLY had something to cry about. I had just been straight-up dumped *on the phone* the night before.

Charlie was all too happy to come to this beautiful girl's rescue. He sat next to her on the bench while she sobbed and wailed, a young Walter Matthau next to the *Planet of the Apes* girl, arm around her and speaking to her in hushed, comforting tones. The crew scattered. "Everyone off the set!" What the hell? I was the one who should have been laid out on the floor!

I had real problems! OK. I went off to my trailer. There I sat, listening to "Nothing Compares 2 U" on steady rotation. I'm not proud to share this fact. If I could have talked to my dumped self with my current wisdom, I would have said, "Turn off that damn song! U R 2 good for this, and he is not the guy 4 U!" but back then I just pressed PLAY for the thirtieth time. I assumed shooting had resumed and I'd be called back in when they needed me. Four hours later, a knock came on the trailer door. "They're ready for you." I went back to the set to learn that nothing had been shot since the morning melt-down. This was a low-budget movie, where every second counts and there's no time or money to spare. But that's the difference between being the beautiful starlet and the best-friend lesbian coffeeshop owner. The starlet shuts down pro-duction for four hours, and the best friend listens to Sinéad O'Connor ad nauseum. Maybe we should have joined forces. For all I know, she may have spent her four hours listening to Sinéad O'Connor too. Dratch 'n' Warren!

This shoot continued with me living in a backdrop of mis-ery. My heart? Broken. My genitals? Viewed. Yes, I was still trying to skillfully avoid College Boy. Well, there was still the work to get me through this, right? The COMEDY?

I failed to mention yet that the plot of the movie involved hottie Estella Warren being a virgin and choosing to which man she would give up her virginity. . . . Yup.

We were filming my last scene. I've been a very stereotypi-cal man-hating lesbian throughout this whole film. My charac-ter had been married to a man in her past. In the last scene, I have a talk with my best friend and roommate Estella Warren.

I had talked to my ex-husband, whom I haven't spoken to for two years.

"Joe called," I say.

"What'd he say?"

"He apologized for driving his truck into the lake. He said he's lonely. "

"Aw, he misses you."

"No, he misses his truck."

We have a little laugh. It was sort of the only grounded moment my character had, with a little joke thrown in for good measure. I was glad to be justifying all my crazy man-hating lines. Right before we were about to shoot, Charlie Matthau came up to me with an excited grin on his face. "Hey! The name Joe isn't funny. So how 'bout if you change it to Abdul!?" He was tickled pink by this idea. "What?" I said. This guy can't be serious. This is the first time you are hearing the name of my ex-husband. It's one of my last scenes. It's a semi-serious moment. Oh, and it's a year after 9/11, when, I hate to say, the only times you were hearing names like Abdul were in connection with terrorism stories on the news. "Why?" "'Cause it's funny!" Now, at that point I should have just said, "No. I'm not doing that." That would have been a page out of the Amy Poehler handbook. She is excellent at shutting people down when she knows better. Not so with myself, back then. "I really don't want to say Abdul." Back and forth we went. "How 'bout Mohammed!?" I can't stress enough how positively deeelighted he was about throwing an unusual, or "funny," name into this scene. Back and forth we went again. I was NOT getting this joke. "How about Ali?" I said, offering up a name to appease this sudden Arab jones he had. For some reason, the name Ali didn't sound as punchline-y-we-are-trying-to-insert-a-wacky-name-here to me. We did one take in which I said Ali. Charlie appeared with a new grin and a brand-new idea. "I got it!" he said. "Say Shaquille." I was dumbfounded. I was frantically searching the set for the writer. "So the audience thinks I was married to Shaquille O'Neal?" "Say it!! Ha-HAAA! Say Shaquille." "I'm not saying Shaquille." I looked to cameramen, to Estella. No one was batting an eye. Where was that damn writer? Then came the most ridiculous suggestion of all. Mind you, I was still fine with JOE. "I got it! I got it! . . . Say . . . O.J.!" So my scene would go "Well. I talked to O.J. . . . He said he misses me." "So . . . ," I said to Charlie while wanting to be ejector-seated off this set and out of Sacramento. "So . . . the audience thinks I was married to O. J. Simpson." "There could be other O.J.'s!" he said through a new round of boyish giggles. "No one is going to think of the 'other' O.J.'s!" Again, why didn't I just take control Poehler-style and say, "We're saying Joe. That's it. Roll cameras." I have no idea! I was trying to bring some integrity to this character, I suppose, and do a good job at playing the best-friend role, but I was at my wit's end. I said, sarcastically and somewhat under my breath, "Why don't we just say Adolf?" "What?" he says. "I said, why don't we just say Adolf?" trying to make him see how crazy his suggestions were. Slight pause. "THAT'S PERFECT! YES! SAY ADOLF!" At this point, I think I simply left my body. At this point, my attempt at biting wit was going to be worked right into the script. At this point, also, I had lost the fight in me. I had gone through Abdul, Mohammed, Shaquille, and O.J., and I happened to check out of the entire process on the name Adolf. So as far as I know (for I have never seen the finished product), in the final cut of the movie, I say, "Well, Adolf called!"

The days were winding down. I'm making this seem like it was a two-month shoot in the desert or something. No, remember, I was there for only two weeks. What more could go wrong?

The final night of shooting! Hooray! Tomorrow I get to go home! I'm sitting in my trailer—we are shooting at night. I hear about five *pops!* like firecrackers. Hmm. About fifteen minutes later, a knock on the trailer door. "Hey, we're escorting everyone to set. There was just a homicide around the corner." Ta-daa!

But there is one more addendum. Another cherry on the grim sundae that was this shoot. We finished at five A.M. They were going to give me a ride back to my hotel. Who should appear to drive me back to the hotel but Bush Viewer!? NOOOO! I had skillfully avoided him for the *entire* shoot— *two whole weeks* and I hadn't seen him again. Now I got to bookend the whole experience with an awkward and silent car ride in the wee hours of the morning for my final moment.

When I left New York for Sacramento, I had high hopes of finally graduating to the best-friend role. Instead I was faced with a straight-to-video experience that included accidental exposure, an on-set meltdown, a clash on the finer points of what's in a name, and a homicide. And when I left New York for Sacramento, I had a boyfriend, albeit an all-wrong-for-me, introduced-me-as-Rachel-not-my-girlfriend-Rachel kind of boyfriend. I returned home from Sacramento to New York as a single woman. I'd have to regroup and eventually turn off the Sinéad O'Connor. Maybe down the road was that perfect movie role for me that could break me through to a whole new level. And maybe down the road I'd find a nice guy who I thought was fantastic and who, just as importantly, felt the same about me. I believe this was the point at which I swore off dating the actors and comedians and the charismatic performers. I didn't need that anymore. All I needed was a regular Joe . . . or Abdul (hee-heeee!) . . . or Mohammed (haaa-haaa!) . . . or Shaquille (bwahh haaa-haaaaaa!). . . .

Hey, Baby!

Back to my dating crusade, and trying to keep hope alive: The third date that came my way was with a man I met doing a night of new screenplay readings. He was the producer of the evening. I had been invited to a friend's party afterward that was going to be my usual crowd—the marrieds and gays. But this was the new, proactive Rachel who opts to go out with the group of people from the reading! We all went out to a bar, and the producer and I chatted the night away. This guy was cute, age appropriate, smart, creative, seemed fun, no ring. . . . I referred to him as the Hot Nerd.

Hot Nerd thought I might be right for another reading he was producing about a month later, so we exchanged info. The next day, he called and we chitchatted. Kinda flirty. Shy, retiring, I was ready to hang up after the basics had been exchanged, but Hot Nerd kept the conversation going. He asked how an audition went that I had mentioned. We talked about that. Chatted some more. He told me more about the upcoming reading. And then? . . . We hung up. That was that. Gone were the days when I would ever ask a guy to do something. If a guy was really interested, he would find a way. I immediately gave up on the idea of Hot Nerd.

About a month later, Hot Nerd called back to give me an update on the reading. We chatted some more about this and that. At the end of the conversation, there was a bit of a pause. "Well, we should go get a drink sometime," he said.

Did Hot Nerd just ask me out? Yes, I think he did! "Yeah, sure!" I said. I was leaving town for a week, so I told him I'd call him when I got back. When I returned, I gave Hot Nerd a call. I got his voice mail and left a message, your standard "Hey, I'm back in town, so give me a call." A week went by. Hmm. A whole week. At this point, picture in your mind the frame of a house sitting quietly and then picture a single beam falling off of it and swinging, perhaps with a cartoon sound effect. That's what happened in my mind when he took a week to call back.

When he called back, he left a message on my voice mail. When I listened to this message, I was walking down a loud New York street—so loud that I couldn't quite make out the voice mail he had left, which was a bit garbled anyway. All I heard was "Hey just checking in" or something like that. I went straight to a hair appointment I had. I texted him back. "Hey, I'm getting my hair cut but will call you in a bit." I was going to be leaving town for another week, so I should see this guy soon, before any momentum wore off. He texted me back. "I thought we agreed only I could cut your hair." Flirty! Cute! Random! I called back, got voice mail, and said, "Hey, I'm actually leaving town again. I don't know what your tomorrow looks like, but I'm free then."

He didn't call back. Two days passed. Another beam falls off the house. I was leaving town that day and I needed to look up a phone number that I had saved in my voice mail, so I listened to my saved messages. Oh! What do ya know? I had saved that garbled message from when I was walking down the street. Only now that I was in my apartment, I could hear it a little more clearly.

"Hi, Rachel. Sorry it took me a while to get back to you. I had a baby a couple days ago BLAH BLAH BLAH WHITE NOISE WHITE NOISE WHAT THE @&*&^%!!!"

No. I could not have heard that correctly. I actually thought, wait a minute, he's a producer and writer; he was probably referring to some project he was working on, like "I've been so busy working on this thing, it's my baby!" I listened again. Nope. Sure enough. This guy just had a *baby*. ". . . took me a while to get back to you. I had a baby a couple days ago. Well, I didn't have the baby, but it's my baby! So I've been on the front lines here BLAH BLAH BLAH MEOW MEOW."

Oh . . . my . . . God. I was stunned. A baby? This dating thing really wasn't working out at all. I guess this never was a date, was it? Was this one all in my head? Did these guys just want to hang out with someone who had been on *SNL*? Were they interested in me or Lorne Michaels?

In my defense, I don't go through life thinking dudes are hot for me. By this point in my life, I had become quite cynical. When meeting new guys, I would just assume "not interested" or "attached," and move on to a state of pleasant surprise if signs pointed to the contrary. And now, I was learning, signs pointing to the contrary still had to be viewed with a heaping dose of cynicism.

Just to be clear: When someone *asked me out,* I used to assume that meant they were *asking me out.* Between Gay Starf***er and Hot Nerd, I guess that assumption no longer applied.

Even before all this, on the rare occasion when I'd find myself flirting with a cute guy who seemed single, I'd still have my warning systems on for when that G-Bomb might drop. The G-Bomb—he has a Girlfriend.

It could come up sometimes late in the conversation, or even after it had ended. "Hey! That guy George is really nice! He's cute!"

"Yeah!" my friend and eternal wingman, Lisa, would say. "He was totally flirting with you. He told me he likes you."

"Really?"

"Yeah! But I think he has a girlfriend. I don't know what's up with it. All his friends want them to break up, but they're trying to work it out." Blah blah blah blah blah G-BOMB.

If dropped too late in a conversation, the G-Bomb can come with crushing disappointment. I remember the worst case of this in recent memory took place at a film fest. I was talking to this cool guy—a graphic artist who was cute and really laid-back. We were chatting the night away, just the two of us, as other film types buzzed around the party. The summer night air was balmy, the wine was flowing, the stars were out. Graphic Artist was so easy to talk to! In my mind, I was already telling my friends about the cool guy I met at this party. Oh, and my friend who would be joining me at the fest wasn't arriving until the next day, so I was alone at the party. Therefore, I was also already creating the "reward" story in my head, about how if you go somewhere alone and buck your social fear, you will surely meet someone. "Look how great this worked out!" said my optimistic self to my cynical self. About a half hour in, we were discussing travel.

"Oh, you've been to Italy! I love Italy! I was there just last summer!" I said.

"Yeah, my fiancée and I are going there in June."

Your . . . fiancée? Am I hearing things? Did you just jump the G-Bomb and go F-Bomb on me? After I logged a good thirty minutes of scintillating conversation with my flirting A-Game? Granted, my flirting A-Game is another woman's banter when ordering a sandwich at Subway, but I told you, I'm behind the curve on this stuff.

When you are in a *committed* flirting relationship with a guy at a party, and telling your friends about him in your head, and then you hear that word *fiancée*, the F-Bomb—at that point, your brain sends an "Emergency! Emergency!" alarm to your mouth. You have to expertly and swiftly throw a smile onto the projector that is your face.

"Ohhh! You're engaged?! Congratulations! When's the wedding?" when inside, you are saying "AWWWW NO F'ING WAY! ARE YOU F'ING *KIDDING ME*?!"

The fine art of keeping that painted-on congratulatory smile while your innards are imploding is a true skill. This particular time, I felt like I was in a Bugs Bunny cartoon; you know, when your whole body cracks into pieces and slowly falls to the floor in chunks, leaving just a cartoon smile suspended in midair. "Ohhh! You're engaged!? Fantastic!" says the Mouth. Then all your teeth fall out one by one, until just one tooth is left swinging, with a tiny little cartoon swinging noise to accompany it.

Regarding the Hot Nerd: When I finally went to do the reading, I got some interesting scoop quite by accident. I was talking to this woman, and she was speaking very highly of Hot Nerd.

"He's great," she said, in a way that made me think she may have had a crush on him at some point. "Yeah," she went on, "I knew him for, like, four months before I ever found out he had a wife and two kids! These showbiz guys, they like to keep their private life a secret."

AHA! I wanted to scream, stand up, and raise my arms in triumph. Vindication Station!! I wasn't crazy! I was just a hapless casualty in Hot Nerd's MO of reckless flirting. And so, once again, the Rule of Threes kicked in, and my dating crusade came to a disappointing close. I would retreat back into the comfort zone where I concluded I belonged, at least for now. You know what they say: Fool me once, shame on you; fool me three times, ya married gay cannibals, shame on me.

A Real Dog

After the Dating Crusade, I decided to give up on talking to strangers and making an effort and just let things naturally take their course, and wouldn't you know it, I was downright seduced by someone. That's right, it happened when I wasn't looking. Only thing is, he was a real dog. Not a guy like "he's such a dog." I'm talking a black Lab. His name was Burleigh. He started out gently enough, all kisses and romance. As the relationship went on, though, I discovered his dark side. He was prone to mood swings, even violence. In the end, he went back to his old girlfriend.

We met in a vacation spot, where you only see someone's good side. It was Park City, Utah—an idyllic ski town. Burleigh was living there at the time. He was athletic and the mountain air suited him. I was a guest in his home (and the home of his owner, Ida, who was my friend's cousin). Burleigh didn't get a lot of attention in the home. You might say he was completely ignored. I felt pretty bad for him. There was a new baby, and as far as I could tell, Burleigh was crated for much of the day and did not get to enjoy long walks. He was let out for a few moments to do his business and called back in. He slept on a dog bed in the corner. In times of stress, he would eat diapers.

The big thing I noticed was that nobody ever seemed to pet him. Ladies, listen to me good. You'd *best* pay attention to your dogs or they *will* go get it somewhere else. By "it," I mean ear scratching.

The first night, as the evening wound down, I was settled into my guest bedroom, lying in bed in the dark, with a hint of moonlight coming through the window. That's when I heard the door swing open. I felt someone climb onto my bed, oh so brazenly, in spite of the fact that he knew he wasn't allowed! Not on that clean white duvet! But he didn't care. It had been so long since he had felt the human touch.

I was lying on my side, and he came up and lay right next to me. I felt his hot breath as he put his face into mine, with his chin pointed down a bit so he could look right into my eyes. Then, still gazing into my eyes, he actually put his paw on my shoulder, assuming what I would call a lover's pose. I chuckled to myself. Never before had I been embraced by a dog! I wanted to call to my friends so they could check out this scenario, but their rooms were too far away, and besides, it might have ruined the moment. I rolled over on my other side, and Burleigh kept his paw on my shoulder. OK, this was too much. I was being spooned by a dog.

The next morning, the only evidence of our forbidden

encounter was the fact that the duvet cover was completely covered with black strands of fur. I told everyone about this sweet moment and was informed that Burleigh was not supposed to be on the beds. "Uh-huh. Oops. OK," I said, knowing full well that I would be defying that rule. This could be the only loving he got all year, and I secretly knew he had an all-access pass to my boudoir and to my heart.

When we left Park City, I told Ida that if she ever thought dog ownership was too much, I would gladly take him off her hands. She didn't respond, "Absolutely not! He's my best friend!" She actually seemed as if she might consent to Burleigh and me starting our beautiful life together. But it was not to be . . . at that moment.

Two years later, Ida and her family had moved to DC and had another baby. The report came from my friend—"Poor Burleigh!" "What do you mean?" "He's always last man on the totem pole. Strangers pay more attention to him than his own family." Let me add that this friend is extremely stoic and Norwegian. If I may translate from the Norwegian to Emotional Jewish her true meaning: "It's an emergency! You must save him!"

I had a dog, growing up—a collie/shepherd/husky mix who had run up to me on our lawn when I was twelve years old, and we ended up keeping her. In spite of my father's hatred of dogs, he gave it the OK because he could see how attached to her we already were. The first night she was allowed to sleep in our house, she had diarrhea all over the dining room floor. Her rocky beginning notwithstanding, she ended up being the member of the family that was the easiest to get along with, and I think we would all sign on to that statement. Even my dad ended up loving her. She has been gone for more than twenty years now and I still miss her and have dreams about her. So having a dog is something that's always been on my list of life things, except with my long work hours, I never had the time. Now, off of *SNL*, off of *30 Rock*, with few auditions coming in, well, this could be the perfect moment for me to have a dog! I mean, if I were a big *television* star, I'd be too busy for a *dog*, right? Ha-haaa! Take that, Hollywood!

I sent Ida an e-mail—"My offer still stands!" She wrote back that I could take him for a month or two. It would be a summer vacation for Burleigh to get some attention, an experiment perhaps in non-dog-ownership for Ida, and a test run of dog ownership for me. Perhaps I could even look at it as a rent-to-own situation, if things worked out for all parties.

A friend of mine was driving up from DC to NY and so she

brought Burleigh up with her. I went to her apartment to pick him up. She had warned me that he seemed "stressed out." I opened the door. This was not the dog I knew. Crazed and barking, he acted as if he didn't even know me. As if the night we had shared together never even happened. I wanted to tell him, "Look, pal. YOU initiated it. YOU came into my room. YOU were the one with all the slick moves. The paw on the shoulder? One of your patented moves, perhaps?"

I brought him back to my apartment. Gradually, we warmed up to each other as the days and weeks went on. I hadn't counted on the fact that although he was now getting the companionship I assumed every dog would want, he was extremely stressed about being in new surroundings. At his old home, he went for hours without an interaction, but I guess that's how he knew life to be. At least his barking died down, and we went on plenty of long walks together since, like I said, I was a highly unemployed actor at the time. So what else was there to do? He woke me up at six thirty every morning to be fed. Then we'd have the morning walk, the midmorning walk, the long early afternooner, the prenight, and the bedtime walk. He showed a high interest in tracking pigeons and squirrels. As soon as we'd enter the park where these critters resided, he would get extremely excited, as if he was collecting points in a video game for each critter he could charge. At first he slept on the rug next to my bed, but he soon took his place on my bed and yes, quite soon after he moved in, we began sleeping together.

He wasn't as connected as he had been back in Utah. He didn't gaze into my eyes or spoon me. But he would follow me wherever I was going in the apartment and lie at my feet. I realized after we began living together, though, that Burleigh had two sides: the charming side that I saw when we first met and a dark side, the snarling beast that had greeted me at the door . . . the side I referred to as Cujo.

Most of the time when I'd come home, he'd happily run up to greet me, tail wagging. But every once in a while, I would be faced with Cujo. It was truly a Jekyll and Hyde situation. His entire physicality would change. I knew I was dealing with Cujo when I could see the whites of his eyes. That meant he was in crazy mode—disconnected, hyper, spazzy, feral—some vestigial behavior relating to unknown traumas before he landed in an animal shelter as a rescue. "Isn't that so like me?" I thought. Once again I had managed to pick a bad boy with a complicated past who seemed really sweet and nice the first time we met and saved all his bad shit for after we were fully involved.

Then came the day I found out just how dark this Burleigh was. . . .

I ran into my friend Jenny and we were going to hang somewhere near my apartment in the East Village. I just needed to walk the dog. "I love dogs! I'll come with you to walk him!" Jenny is a sweet, wide-eyed dancer who had once done a reading of a musical with me. We arrived at my apartment and right away I saw . . . it's Cujo time. Burleigh was crazed. He was jumping, he was barking like crazy. The whites of his eyes were gleaming in full effect. He was even nipping a bit. We took him out for a walk and he continued to behave like a madman. His barking was not dying down. I ran into a store, and while Jenny had the leash with him outside, he barked loudly nonstop. I came out of the store and we turned off of Houston onto First Street at First Ave. There's a little park there with a wrought-iron fence. I was holding Burleigh's leash pretty closely. "He's not usually this crazy!" I said.

The following happened in a split second: Burleigh thrust his head under the wrought-iron fence in a whir. He emerged with lightning speed; in his jaws, he was holding a pigeon. It was like a city version of a National Geographic film, where out of nowhere the crocodile appears from the water and chomps down on an antelope; only this was the urban jungle and pigeons were the prey.

"Oh my God! He's got a pigeon!" screamed Jenny. Burleigh had finally won his video game. I dropped my bags and was trying to pry his jaws open to free the struggling bird. A small crowd was watching. We were yelling, screaming, "BUR-LEIGH, NO!!" The pigeon's wings were moving in Burleigh's mouth. "There's blood," I said in the clinical voice of a trauma doctor. I was still trying to free the bird. Blood started dripping on the sidewalk. Burleigh would not let go, until finally he did. The pigeon was not quite dead. He was trying to lift his head and move a wing. When I have told this to my friends, some people say, "Well, who needs one more pigeon running around New York!" but I felt really bad for the bird. He was just minding his business in the park. He wasn't even all dirty and scrawny. He was kind of pretty before Burleigh got ahold of him. When Burleigh dropped the bird, Jenny and I just stared at each other. Adrenaline was pumping, I was breathing hard, my hand covered with pigeon blood. I think both of our brains were trying to figure out how to go back in time two minutes and undo what had just happened. Seeing that bird futilely flailing on the sidewalk was a sickening sight for me, and even more so for Jenny, a strict vegetarian who doesn't even eat fish, for humane reasons.

As we stood panting on the sidewalk, out emerged a sort of New York angel. We could have encountered anyone there—a scolder, a laugher, someone to make us feel bad. Instead, a woman came up to us who had seen the incident. She looked a bit like a New York hippie—a bit older than me. In a calm earth-mama voice, she said, "They're animals. That's just their nature. It's what they do. I know it's traumatic to see, but that's just what they do." "Thank you. You're really nice," I said.

I have to confess, I did not look back to see what was up with the bird. I hoped it had died by then for its own sake, but I knew if it hadn't, I didn't have a pioneer woman living inside me who would pick up a brick to do a mercy killing. I'm not a manly woman. I just play them on TV.

We walked the fifteen blocks back to my apartment. Jenny had a large, long spot of pigeon blood on her new jeans. My hand was still covered in it as well. We got to my apartment and without many words, I went into repair mode. We sat on my porch. I robotically brought my speakers out there and flipped immediately to Joni Mitchell and poured some wine as emergency medication.

And there was Burleigh. Now that he had satisfied his quest for blood, he had reverted out of Cujo mode and lay at my feet like something out of a Norman Rockwell painting.

He was calm. He was sweet. What was it with this guy? He could not be controlled! Completely unpredictable! One minute causing me extreme anxiety and distress, the next, a damn dreamboat. I had sworn this inconsistent energy out of my life. IT'S NOT GOOD FOR ME. You hear that, mister? You aren't good for me!! I can't take the chaos!

That night, Burleigh went to assume his sleeping position in my bed.

"No!" I said. "I cannot sleep with you tonight, Burleigh. Your violent tendencies are a reeeal turnoff."

Turns out the decision to keep Burleigh around or send him packing was not mine to make. My assumption that Ida might want to unload him on me turned out to be wrong.

Another friend of Ida's came to pick him up to bring him back to DC. In the moment, I was sad to see him go. I sure wouldn't miss waking up at six thirty A.M. to feed him, but I would miss him settling his head onto my leg when I was lying on the floor watching TV.

I felt bad about the way we said good-bye. One minute he was lying on my bedroom rug next to me, and the next I got the call that the pickup was here. I put on his leash, trying to convey the meaning: This isn't just an ordinary walk; this is good-bye! Needless to say, he didn't get it. When we got to the car, he eagerly jumped into the back. This girl didn't know what she was in for. I had taken him on several car rides, and he had barked ferociously and incessantly for four hours. I tried to warn her. "I'm sure he'll be fine," she said. "Um . . . yeah. I don't know," I said in a high, falsely optimistic voice. I handed her a bottle of wine. "Here. You might need this when you get home."

I went back into my apartment. It had an empty feeling. The only reminder of Burleigh was the mountains and mountains of black fur that were all over my floors and bed. Countless Swifferings brought him back into my life in the weeks to follow. I guess I wasn't cut out for dog ownership, at least on my own. I hadn't taken into account that when we had my childhood dog, there were four of us to take care of her. I imagined having a dog would enhance my life: There I am, coming home from a night out, being greeted by the ol' lovebug! Oh! Now I'm hanging out at the dog park, talking to the cute guy with the boxer after our leashes get tangled! Now I'm on the beach on Cape Cod, tossin' Burleigh the tennis ball! In actuality, Burleigh tied me to my apartment much more than I would have liked, because I felt too guilty leaving him alone for any length of time.

Here's a secret: I had to admit to myself that somewhere deep inside, I was looking at this experiment in dog ownership as practice for "What if I ever wanted to have a baby on my own?" I would never have voiced this to a soul, but it was a tiny thought in my head. I mean, the dating wasn't working out—and I was in my early forties. I had to think about these things, though I seldom did. Was the fact that I was relieved to unload Burleigh back on his owners proof that I was too focused on myself to care for another being? Did I care more about hanging out with the funniest of friends and comedians over a bottle of Montepulciano and a bowl of tagliatelle Bolognese than I did about nurturing a tiny human life? (I'm talking delicious and expertly made tagliatelle Bolognese, so take that into account.)

It was a distinct possibility.

Attack of the Tiny Pants

I never liked going to baby showers. Here are people who like baby showers: women in their twenties, grandmas-to-be, people who already have babies, people who love to look at Stuff. These are the Shower People.

Here are people who hate baby showers: women in their late thirties to early forties who think they might want kids but haven't met the right guy yet, aka me. Also people who don't like looking at Stuff and having to pass it around and say, "Ohhhhhh! It's a shirt! Only it's a tiny shirt!" or "Ohhhhhh! It's pants! Only they're tiny!" aka me. This deadly combo made me really have to steel myself to go to a baby shower.

Back when I was on *SNL*, I went to one very fancy shower that took place on my one day off, a precious Sunday afternoon. The guest of honor was about an hour and a half late, so all the small talk had been small-talked. It was a huge shower and there was a mountain of gifts. And this mom-to-be was going SLOWWWLY. When the first item was opened and about fifteen minutes was spent slowly passing it around, with everyone commenting on it, I felt a wave of rising panic set in. I looked at the mountain of gifts. Let's see, fifteen minutes per gift times what looks to be fifty gifts. Oh my God! I could be here for *five* hours. And I was.

This was when I still had "plenty of time" to have a baby, before I hit my forties and my own personal panic that I might never have a child was thrown in for good measure. This was just my Anti-Shower Baseline.

In addition to the mini clothes and smiling stuffed animals, there was also this category with which to contend: things you've never heard of and have no idea what they do that start a big discussion among the mommies in the group. I would sit quietly as a chorus of mommies oooed and aaahhed over things I didn't even know existed.

"Ohhhhhh! Yes. You're going to NEED that."

"The Nipple Prepper. I used it all the time."

"I would have been LOST without the Nipple Prepper."

"YOU NEED TO HAVE THE NIPPLE PREPPER!"

Next gift. A Red Tent howl of excitement rises up among the mommies.

"Aghhhhh! Yes! The Swaddling Wizard. Oh my God! That was invaluable to me when I had Maddie."

"You cannot LIVE without the Swaddling Wizard."

"The doctor told me if I hadn't used the Swaddling Wizard, Logan would have ended up on the spectrum."

Next gift . . . Tiny Dress. AHHHHH! AWWWW! NOOO! OHHHHHH! OOOOOOOH! HOLY FUCKING SHIT! IT'S A DRESS BUT IT'S TINY! IT HAS A DAMN BEAR ON IT! WOOOOOOOAAAAAHHHH!

These showers were getting tougher for me with the increasing realization that I would probably not be having kids, but when I was invited to a baby shower for some of my best friends, David and Russell, I wouldn't have dreamed of missing it. David was one of the Dartmouth in-the-closet-during-school-out-after-graduation crowd. David and Russell met right after David had graduated college. They had been together for twenty-plus years and they had just adopted a baby, so this shower took place after little Sadie had been born. The shower was coed, which made it easier (cuts down on the ooo-aaahh factor by quite a bit). While I was there, I bumped into a college classmate whom I knew enough to greet but not enough to do any serious cooing over the new baby he was holding.

"Hi! Who's this?" I said halfheartedly.

"This is Sam. He's six weeks old."

"Awwww," I said, like the trained monkey I had become when looking at babies to whom I have no connection. Sam produced a smile.

"Oh, just look at him," says new dad. "*Is there anything better than this?*"

And congratulations! Ding Ding Ding!! (Balloon drop/confetti) You have just won the contest of "Things not to say to a forty-two-year-old single woman who is spending her Sunday afternoon at a baby shower." *Is there anything better than this?* No. That's what I keep hearing over and over again and that's what I'm "missing out on" and the whole world has babies and it's *the* life experience and if you don't have it, YOU SHOULDN'T EVEN BOTHER TO LIVE BECAUSE THERE ISN'T ANY-

THING BETTER THAN THIS AND OH! IT'S TIME TO
GATHER 'ROUND AND LOOK AT TINY PANTS!

I just wasn't one of those women who would want to have a child on her own. I knew I wasn't cut out for the sperm bank or solo adoption. Motherhood was something I had always imagined for myself, but I didn't think of myself as a "baby person," the first one to say "Ohhhhhh! Can I hold your babyyyy?" when a friend had a child. If I found a partner, yes, I definitely wanted kids. But here I was at forty, forty-one, forty-two, now forty-three. I kept moving up the window of fertility and possibility, trying to block out the statistics with which I was bombarded, but to be realistic, I started to adjust to the fact that I wasn't having kids. I was trying genuinely and oh so gradually to become OK with that; I had to focus on the benefits of my life. Some friends' marriages were beginning to crumble and other friends were completely consumed with shuttling to soccer games and swim meets, while in my jet-set lifestyle, I was flying off to the Caribbean for a last-minute getaway or to Burning Man to see old-man dicks.

Sure, I'd still have mornings where I'd wake up thinking, "Wow. I may be alone forever and never have a family. I may miss out on a really big LIFE THING," which could create a rising panic in me. But for the most part, I realized that as we grow older, we adjust and roll with what we have in the present, though it may not be the future we had dreamed up for ourselves in the past. I was forty-three years old and I was actually seeing the benefits of not having kids and was accepting my fate after all those years of struggling.

Then, I met a guy in a bar.

Girl Walks into a Bar

On a Sunday night at the beginning of summer in New York City, I went out with my friend Lisa. Lisa is a total New York City character, the unofficial mayor of the Lower East Side. I met her back when she was the bartender at my favorite New York restaurant, and we eventually struck up a friendship. She is brash and loud at times, but she also has a surprising wisdom about human behavior, like a stereotypical bartender you'd see in a movie. Lisa has long black hair and a complexion so pale it tips the fact that she rarely ventures out in daytime. She knows her wine very well, maybe too well, in fact. The woman likes to drink. I remember one time she said she was giving up drinking.

"You are?" I said, totally shocked.

"Yeah," she said in complete seriousness, "I'm only drinking white wine."

Lisa is also best kept in the ten-block radius of her neighborhood. One of the only times we lured her out of her turf, she came to see the live show of *SNL*. At the after-party, she approached Dennis Haysbert, who had done a guest spot on the show. He is perhaps best known as the Allstate Insurance guy, though also a legit actor whom I knew of from the movie *Far from Heaven*. Lisa started talking to him and cornered the guy for about twenty minutes. He was completely gracious about it, but from then on, we realized we had to be careful when we took Lisa out of her usual society of ne'er-do-wells and oddballs. "I'm inviting Lisa to this party," I'd say to Daisy. "But keep an eye on her and don't let her Haysbert anyone."

Lisa was pretty much always up for going out on the town at a moment's notice. She is gay and practically the only person with whom I manage to meet guys, because she literally forces me to talk to them whether I want to or not. She usually facilitates conversation, then ditches me with the guy, often someone I have no interest in speaking with, saying, "I'LL JUST LEAVE YOU TWO TO GET BETTER ACQUAINTED!" or some other subtle phrase such as that. When I don't feel like chatting up strangers and I try to object, Lisa will usually come back at with me a loud "Step *away* from the lesbian!"

This particular night, I suggested we go to Zum Schneider, a fun outdoor beer joint that's conveniently located near her apartment, but to my surprise she texted back, "Let's go to Shoolbred's," a bar near my apartment. So I met her at Shoolbred's. We sat outside, but the waiter was taking a really long time to come out and take our order that night, so I went in to order for us at the bar. I walked up to the bar, and a man standing next to me turned to me and said, "Hey, we're about to order absinthe. Have you ever tried it?"

"Uch! Don't do it!" I said. "That stuff is disgusting!"

The only other time I had tried absinthe was with Horse-meat, and we all know how that one turned out. I talked to Absinthe Man, whose name I learned was John, while I waited for my order. He told me he worked for a wine company and was in New York on business for a food show. He was there with his niece and her boyfriend, who lived across the street. He was from Northern California, which was a strange coincidence because a mere three days before, I had gotten desperate enough to start browsing on Match.com. Oh, I wasn't bold enough to take action or ever create a profile. I was just window-shopping. I checked out the New York offerings and couldn't imagine myself with any of them. I thought of the guys in Northern California—how I always find cute guys there with varied interests who are so much more down-to-earth than New York actors I had encountered. So a mere three days before I met John, I had been looking at Match.com San Francisco, and now here I was meeting a handsome, friendly, funny guy from the Bay Area. *Universe??*

After only about fifteen minutes of conversation, he asked me when I was coming to visit him in California. I had to go back to Lisa at our table outside, but I told them to come join us out there and they did. He was quite forward, telling Lisa right in front of me, "I think your friend is cute." Of course he had to check with her first on the sly to make sure we weren't a couple—that's the drawback of having a lesbian as your wingman.

Only a few minutes after John and company joined our table, we had a jarring New York Moment. I find New York City to be a pretty friendly place, and to me, once you know your way around, it feels like a big neighborhood. I've rarely run into any "crazies." We were sitting at the table and a man was walking by with two large dogs pulling at their leashes. I first noticed him because of the unusual dogs—they were straight-up hound dogs, a rare sighting in Manhattan. The man looked to be in his mid-fifties with a gray crew cut and black-rimmed glasses and shorts. As he walked by the table, he leaned in and, out of nowhere, *screamed* at us, "YOU'RE ALL A BUNCH OF COCKSUCKERS!" The dogs reared up on their hind legs and started barking like the animal henchmen who accompany the villain in a Disney movie. We were so shocked, we practically choked on our drinks, not knowing whether to giggle or "throw down." (Not that I've ever "thrown down." Which you can tell because I put it in quotes.) Then he looked right at me. He looked straight into my eyes and said, "AND YOU! YOU'RE A F***ING C***!"

Well! That was . . . um . . . wow. Strange scenario to be in with someone you just met. We all had a shocked laugh about it. I wanted to apologize for my city the way you would for an embarrassing relative. "I swear, New York *never* acts like this. I don't know what New York's problem is—usually, New York is really nice, seriously!"

I didn't think John knew who I was from TV. If he did, he didn't let on. Later in the evening, someone walking by asked to take my picture, I think, but the moment just came and went without discussion. I later found out John did know who I was but also that he didn't have a TV. So he had a vague idea of me but wasn't such a fan he was going to barrage me with questions: "So! Who was the worst host?"

John was going to be in town for one more night. He walked me back to my apartment. "Am I going to see you again before I leave?" he asked me, so I invited him to come out with a group of friends who were going to dinner the next night.

He arrived at dinner bearing bacon-flavored lip balm for all, from the food show he had attended earlier that day. This guy could be a winner. We broke off from the group after the meal and hit another bar and then he walked me back to my place. "You can come up," I said, "but let's not go apeshit." The next day, John had to go to the food show to work. He had mentioned that in addition to selling wine from New Zealand, his company also sold New Zealand mussels, but the mussels weren't selling as well. In the morning, we were joking around about how he could get the mussels to sell better. I was picturing him bounding out onto the demo area, wearing a foam mussel headpiece for a costume, with one of those headset microphones, clapping his hands over his head as the song "Y'all ready for this? ba ba bum BA BA bum, bum bum bum bum BA BA ba bum bum bum bum" played overhead. We started laughing at this vision and ended up laughing so hard, we couldn't breathe and had tears streaming down our faces. I admit this may have been one of those "you had to be there" moments, but I registered at the time that it's pretty rare to have a laughing fit like that with someone you just met.

"You should come to Mill Valley this weekend for July Fourth."

"You're joking, right?" I asked him.

"NO! We'd have a blast."

That was too crazy for me. I had known him for two days at

that point. No, I couldn't just up and visit him in California that very weekend. After he went back, he sent me cute and funny texts over the next few days, making sure to bring up July Fourth. I thought about the holiday weekend I had planned—Shelter Island with a fun group of friends—but it was my same old deal: me with some couples, a few single ladies, and absolutely no prospects. Maybe it was time for me to take some radical action. I think another factor was a failed setup that had just occurred, where this guy and I had been e-mailing back and forth for about a month but I had been out of town so much that, by the time we were supposed to meet, he had met someone else. That was fresh in my mind regarding John, who lived in California. A few days before July Fourth, I asked John, "Are you still serious about me visiting?"

"Yes! I'll fly you out here."

"You don't have to fly me out there."

"If you're gonna spend five hours on a plane to see me, I'm flying you out here," he insisted. "Weird," I thought. "This must be what chivalry feels like."

I got on the plane, propelled by a heady mix of curiosity, adventurousness, and post–Dating Crusade, single-lady desperation. I had always had an impulsive side, which made this seem kind of crazy but not entirely out of my wheelhouse. Somewhere in the back of my head must have been the thought that No leads to dead ends, and Yes leads to possibilities. Again, hearkening back to my improv days, this was the ultimate "Yes And."

John picked me up at the San Francisco airport. The visit

did not start off seamlessly, since I was on the wrong level and we kept having to call each other and I was saying, "I'm on level 2," when actually I was on level 1. Already, this was not the movies. Once we connected and I got into his car, we enjoyed an extremely awkward ride back to his house. When I'd met him in New York, he was all confidence, but in the car, he seemed nervous, and that made *me* nervous. We struggled for small talk, with silences filling the air. Internally, I started to panic, thinking, "What the HELL am I doing here? Screw 'Yes And.' That's a horrible concept!" His place was a nice town house with bachelor-pad style—not a lot of furniture, just the basics. Like I said, he didn't have a TV. He would watch documentaries on Netflix instead. (That automatically meant he used his time more wisely than I, who have my TV on Bravo 24/7, squandering my time with *Real Housewives*.) We had to resort to cracking open a bottle of wine when I arrived—yes, at the extremely early happy hour of one P.M.—to ease our fear, but we ended up getting over our nerves, and I actually felt more comfortable with him as the weekend went on. Not fully comfortable—I had a baseline of nervousness that made me barely eat the whole time. This trend would soon reverse when we got to know each other better and he dubbed me The Crow for the way I picked apart my food as well as the remnants of his, leaving behind a plate that looked as if a bird had landed on it.

John was a very sweet planner and tour guide, offering all sorts of options for the weekend. We ended up going to a few parties—one at the home of a friend of his and one that we were invited to by one of the Dartmouth Gays—an annual Pork-Off party where people competed in cooking various pork dishes. We all had to submit a "porku"—a haiku we wrote about pork. John showed me around San Francisco, a city in which I hadn't spent much time. We stopped at the marine mammal rehab center and looked at the seals. That trip was slightly interrupted because John also worked for a vitamin company and had taken a B vitamin with a "niacin shot" when we were leaving his house. I took one too—what the heck— and partway through the marine center, my face started to feel hot. I looked in the mirror, and my face, neck, and hands had turned bright red. I was having some sort of allergic reaction to the vitamin. My bright red, burning tomato face lasted about a half hour. It was a bit embarrassing but more funny than anything else. I mean, once you've been called a f***ing c*** in front of someone, the bar of social awkwardness has been set pretty high.

A whole weekend date with someone you don't know all that well can be intense and nerve-racking and fun all rolled into one. John commented that we were experiencing the "waterboarding" of dating, and I had to agree. The next time I saw him, he had a gift for me. . . . He had tracked down a T-shirt that said I'D RATHER BE WATERBOARDING.

After the July Fourth weekend, John and I continued our long-distance, casual, fun, not-defined relationship. We talked on the phone pretty much every day. He definitely acted like he was courting me. He'd text "I miss you! Wish you were here!" I really wasn't used to this dynamic at all—being pursued instead of feeling like the pursuer. A month later, he came to New York and accompanied me to Fire Island, where I was doing an ensemble comedy show that I do from time to time. It's always a hit—always gets laughs—but wouldn't you know it, on this particular occasion, the first time he was ever seeing me perform, the show completely bombed. I was mortified. I sheepishly skulked up to him after the show and had to trot out the old Second City improv line: "This is usually really funny! I swear!"

As the cross-country visits continued, we would usually end up having a few major laughing fits together. He continued his surprise acts of chivalry and sweetness. When I went to wine country with my friends and happened to mention to him the wine we liked best, a wine I had never heard of from a tiny family vineyard, a case of it arrived at my apartment a week later. He had ice cream in his freezer called Three Twins, and when I tried it, I exclaimed, "Oh my God, this is some of the best ice cream I've ever tasted!" Wouldn't you know it, six pints arrived in New York on dry ice. (Have you noticed a food and wine theme here?) He was always planning our next adventure. "Come meet me in Chicago!" he'd say when he had a meeting there. He came to Manhattan in September for a few weeks and stayed in a friend's vacant apartment because "he'd always wanted to live in New York at some point," but it sure seemed like he was coming east to hang with me.

Gore vs. W

📺

Our relationship was perfect for two people in their early forties who lived in two different cities. We both liked doing the same sort of things—travel, food, wine, nature. I wasn't sure that on a soul level we were connected. I don't think either of us was, like, "I've found the One!!" but neither of us was too concerned about that fact. It was enough to have a fun "date" and a nice guy to pal around with. There was no pressure to think of "Where is this going?" since it hadn't been going very long at all.

In many ways, we were quite different. He's a Midwesterner who was raised in a devout Catholic family and went to a small business college in Michigan that he calls "one step above DeVry." I'm your typical East Coast gal from the burbs. John told me his dad is so devout that he goes to the church to babysit the statues a few times a week. I thought this was a euphemism of some sort—that he stopped by to make sure everything looked cool, but no—he actually goes and sits with the statues. Aside from the religious differences, though, John possesses a lot of the qualities that I had on my "list." I put the word *list* in quotes so you don't think I'm one of those women who actually wrote out a list, but the truth is I did, so in reality those quotes are a bit of a lie.

John was funny, smart, handsome, very fun, generous, extremely thoughtful, around my age, open to meeting my friends, liked to travel—the list goes on and on. About a month or so after I met him, we were talking on the phone and something about politics came up. John made some comment that sounded a bit right wing to me—I think it may have been something positive about George W. Bush.

"Whooooa. Hold up, hold up, hold up," I said.

"What is it?"

"ARE YOU A . . . REPUBLICAN?!!" I nearly shouted in a shrill tone.

Slight pause. "No. I'm an Independent."

"BULLSHIT!" I cried. "YOU'RE A REPUBLICAN!"

Oh . . . my . . . God. I was dating a *Republican*!? HOW did this HAPPEN!!!? "OK," I said. "Even if you are a Republican, you *have* to admit that George Bush is an idiot."

John proceeded to list some of the "good things" George Bush had done. "UGH! I can't *believe* this!" I was practically hyperventilating.

"Wow," marveled John. "You're really getting angry about this!"

OK. Reel it in, Dratch. He was right. He wasn't getting angry that I was a flaming liberal. Yes, he would call me Al Gore when I insisted on recycling. Yes, he would later soundly mock me when I actually brought home empty plastic bottles in my suitcase after we were in a place where recycling wasn't available. But doesn't he know that there's an ISLAND OF PLASTIC THE SIZE OF TEXAS FLOATING IN THE DAMN PACIFIC OCEAN!?!! Deep breath. Anyway, he wasn't getting worked up because I was a flaming liberal. Yet here I was, having a conniption fit that he was an "Independent." (It can't be true. I *know* he's a Republican!) When I hung up, I had to give myself a talking-to. "Look, you haven't dated anyone seriously in about five years. You're not going to be able to have *every-thing* on your 'list' (again with the quotes)." But that was the thing I realized. I hadn't even put Democrat on my list. Most everyone I know is a Democrat, with the exception of two girl-friends with whom I avoid talking politics entirely. Thus it's kind of my own fault for not writing *exactly* what I wanted on the list. So I just don't really discuss politics with John. I tried to venture there, on a topic I thought surely everyone could agree on. "I'm really upset about this oil spill," I said. "Yeah," he replied, "and the Obama administration waited, like, a week to really respond to the problem." OH! YOU MEAN THE "PROBLEM" THAT BP CREATED AND HAD NO BACKUP EMERGENCY PLAN AND NOW HERE WE WERE A MONTH LATER AND THERE WAS NO SOLUTION IN SIGHT? But I didn't say that. I noted my increased blood pressure and heart rate, remained silent, and thought, "From now on, I'll just talk about this stuff with my other friends."

Meet Me on the Astral Plane

In spite of our outward differences, John and I seemed connected on some sort of psychic level. Sometimes our connection on the spiritual plane gave me pause and made me think I shouldn't take our connection on this plane so lightly. When I went to San Francisco the second time, we were staying at a hotel across from the food and wine fest where we were spending the weekend. When we awoke in the morning, I was aware that I had had some really bizarre dreams, some so bizarre I certainly wouldn't have shared them. Namely, I had dreamed of a detached penis. It was the first and only detached penis dream I could recall ever having in my life.

"I had a really weird dream last night," said John.

"Really? So did I," I said. "What did you dream?"

"Well," said John, "I dreamed of . . . a detached penis."

Oh . . . my . . . God. I looked at him with wide eyes. "NO WAY. *I* HAD A DREAM OF A DETACHED PENIS!!"

"WHAT!?"

"YES!! A DETACHED PENIS! I'VE NEVER HAD A DREAM OF A DETACHED PENIS IN MY LIFE!"

The penii played different roles in our dreams. In his dream, we were in a car and we were pulled over by the cops. The cop, who, because this was a dream, was of course represented by Gary Busey, was saying, "You two are in big trouble!" and he was waving around a detached penis like a weapon. He was waving it in my face and threatening me with it, and John was trying to intervene. In my dream, there was a detached penis lying on the bed and it belonged to my old boyfriend. I was wondering if I could keep it for future use or if anyone would know I took it or if I would get in trouble for that. I don't know—both dreams involved consequences and getting into trouble and . . . a detached penis. Though I did minor in psychology, I can't really crack the code on this one. Maybe if I had majored in it, I could.

Since that happened, I would check to see if any of our dreams matched up again. When we were saying good night on the phone, I'd say, "OK. See you on the astral plane!" I didn't see him on the astral plane until several months later, when we were on a trip together. When we awoke, I realized I had had a ton of vivid dreams that night. I mentioned this to John. "Did you have any?"

"No," he said. "Actually, I was awake at, like, four A.M., and I realized I left my blue fleece jacket on the plane."

I stopped in my tracks. I clenched his arm.

"Oh my God! No way!" I cried.

"What?"

"I have chills!"

"What?! What?!"

"I dreamed that I was holding a blue fleece jacket, one that really exists in my apartment, and I was offering it to you, saying, 'Is this yours? Does this belong to you?'"

In November, John e-mailed me to say, "I have a business meeting in Florida. You could come down and meet me on such-and-such a date. Or . . . Kauai, December 18–27."

These were some grand plans. I'd never been to Hawaii. It seemed very honeymoony. Maybe we weren't serious enough to take that kind of trip together. If I had been in my early thirties, I would have asked myself things like *"Where is this going? What are the implications of this? Is this too big a move?"* But when you're forty-three, you're like, *"Who cares? I've never been to Hawaii. I have fun with this guy. I'm going."*

Kauai was so beautiful that my mind couldn't comprehend it was real. On a hike, we would joke that we were going to look down and see an electrical outlet coming out of the rocks and realize we were just in some Disney World exhibit. We hung out on a private beach in the company of a monk seal and went on hikes through the otherworldly beauty. A truly bizarre thing was there were paparazzi on this remote nature trail following us to take pictures of . . . me? I wanted to tell them— "Guys! Save your energy! These pictures might fetch about two dollars on the mainland!" But other than that, all was very idyllic. Although John did manage to step on a sea urchin and we had to go to the ER to remove the pieces from his foot. The trip had it all—nature, beauty, romance, and a little bit of danger, and it was all because I had said yes when John asked me to go to San Francisco for July Fourth and had said yes to Hawaii and didn't listen to some dumb rules in my head about convention and what you *should* do.

Around the New Year, back in New York, I was having a wicked case of PMS that I just couldn't shake. The *P* of *premenstrual* kept on and on, with the *M* not happening. Then it occurred to me: *I'm going through menopause.* My mother had early menopause at age forty-one, so once I hit forty, I was always aware that it could be coming at any time. I looked up *menopause* on the Internet, curious whether raging PMS was a symptom. I called my friend Megan, one of my childhood friends from home. I have a group of friends I've known since I was a kid, and we all form a circle of amateur therapists, there at the ready for any problem that may arise. "How do I know if I'm going through menopause?" Ugh. I was feeling down. I knew it was a big change for anyone, but when you don't have kids, it seems especially depressing and final.

"What are your symptoms?" she asked me, and I told her about the wicked PMS.

"Well, you could be pregnant."

"That's not possible."

First of all, there was the aforementioned early menopause in my genetic code. Also, there was the simple fact of my age. As any lady knows, you are constantly bombarded by the media and medical establishment with how difficult it can be to conceive after forty. At forty-three, two months shy of forty-four, forget it. It was impossible. I would need medical intervention to get pregnant at my age, and even then it'd probably take a miracle.

I went to class at the gym and started musing, *What if I were pregnant? Was there any way? Maybe I should just get a test to rule it out—a mere formality.* I went to the drugstore after my class. The lady checking me out picked up the pregnancy test and said, "Shee-it. These scare me. I don't even want to *look* at that!"

"I don't think there's anything to worry about," I said, oversharing with my local cashier.

I went home and immediately peed on the stick. I'd never done this before, never even had a scare. I wasn't even the least bit nervous about the outcome. Three minutes later, I went back to check the results. With no ceremony, no heart racing, no sloooow lifting of the stick to grandly eye the results, I picked up the stick, ready to check this off my list as a possibility. Two lines, OK, that must mean "not pregnant." I looked at the guide. Two lines . . . pregna—. . . WHAT? And then, my heart did start racing. I began to pace around the apartment and speak aloud to myself, "Ohmygodohmygodohmygod!"

I frantically called Megan back. No answer. *Nooo!* I called another friend from the Lexington gang. "Debbie!" I say as if I'm being murdered.

"What? What is it?"

"No, it's nothing bad." Mid-hyperventilation. "I'm pregnant!"

If you looked at my Internet history that day, it would read:

"menopause," "menopause symptoms," "signs of menopause," and then "effects of alcohol consumption in early pregnancy."

There were two lines on the stick. In the first hours and even the first week, I was just numb. I was incredulous. I didn't have my wits about me to feel anything. After all the time I'd spent worrying about not having kids, now I felt the sly ol' Universe had just pulled the ultimate fast one on me. Or that somewhere up there, God was chuckling. Not the Judeo-Christian God but some impish god from Greek mythology, rubbing his hands together mischievously. I could not comprehend the news because I had already written my own story—my negative story, mind you—and typeset it in permanent ink. After telling a few other Lexington friends—all of whom were joyous and laughing and happy for me—I now had to tell John. We had known each other for six months at this point, but we had probably spent a total of one month actually in each other's presence. I had to tell John that he might be a father and that there was a possibility that, in some fashion, we would be tied together for life.

I called him up and tried sounding nonchalant.

"Hey! Where are you?"

"I'm driving home from work," he said.

"OK!" said the chipmunk who had taken control of my voice. "Just call me when you get home!"

I wanted him to be sitting down when I gave him the news, and in a stationary location, not behind the wheel of a moving vehicle. He called me back when he arrived home.

"What's up?"

"Um . . ." I started to feel like I was going to hyperventilate again. "I don't know, um, how to say this, but, uh, I was late, uh, with my period, and I just took a test and it said I was pregnant."

John's initial response was skepticism at the idea that a home pregnancy test was completely reliable information. He told me to try the test again, which I'd have to do the next morning. I said, "It's just peeing on a stick. I think it's going to come out the same. I think this is real," but I agreed to try again. Coincidentally, I already had a doctor's appointment scheduled for two days hence, so until we got the official word, John still believed in the idea of a false positive. He was in as much numbness and shock as I was. We weren't used to discussing serious topics—this was all Fun! Light! Merriment! I did the second test: positive. When I went to the doctor the next day, it was confirmed. In a month, I would be forty-four years old, and I was pregnant.

This Little Piggy

◆—●

We had had a warning that this would happen. We had just forgotten about it. Right away when I met John for the first time on his New York trip, within only two days of knowing each other, we realized that we were seeing pigs everywhere, so much so that we both commented on it. Here is a small sampling: As I mentioned, John brought bacon lip balm to the dinner the night he met me out with my friends. When he came to my apartment, the movie *The Amityville Horror* was on TV, and I said, "Oh! This is the one with Jodie the pig." (Jodie was the scary six-foot pig that looked in the family's windows.) Later, John called my feet hamhocks. I'm not proud of that. After we went out to dinner with my friends on the second night, we had gone to the bar Bourgeois Pig. And across the street from Shoolbred's, the bar where we met, there is a huge pig painted on the apartment building where his niece was living with her boyfriend. There was the Pork Off in San Fran on July Fourth weekend, with the porku poems. And when John came back to visit a month later, we were standing on the train platform, and a guy came up to me and said, "I worked on *The Martha Stewart Show* when you were a guest and you made a ham with her." John and I turned to each other and exclaimed, "What is with these pigs?" There's a text service called KGB to which you can text any question and they will write you back with an answer. So we were on the train and John texted, "What is the symbolism of a pig?" He received an answer back in a few moments. "Oh my God," he said, chuckling.

"What does it say?"

He held up his phone for me to see. I looked at the word on the screen: *Fertility.*

At the time, I was almost embarrassed. I let it go right by because I was thinking, "I just started dating this guy. I'm forty-three. I don't think we have to worry about that." It wasn't the kind of thing you want to stress to someone you've just started seeing. What was I going to say? "Well, we don't have to worry about that. Hahaha! I'm TOO OLD!"

So a mere six months later, when I discovered I was pregnant, I thought, "The PIGS! The pigs predicted it! I didn't listen to the pigs!"

Serious with a Capital S

●—●

Before this bombshell, John and I had never had to discuss anything Serious with a capital *S* before. The biggest decisions we were making as any sort of couple were what vacation to go on or what wine to order. I think we were both now mildly terrified. To me, I had a miracle on my hands and yet, it was scaring the hell out of me. I knew in my heart I would go forward with having the baby. Even though I had thought I would never have a baby alone, I felt like I'd won some odd lottery and I was going to go with what the Fates/She-Wolf Goddess/Hawaiian Volcano gods or the Universe had determined for me. I didn't know what John would do. He said all the right things. "We're in this together, we'll get through this." We hadn't even seen each other in person yet. Some nights on the phone, I would get so scared I would cry. He would calm me down. Other nights, he would be the one freaking out and I would be the soother. I told him I was going forward with the birth and that he could be as involved or uninvolved as he wanted to be.

We finally saw each other in person about two weeks after I learned of the pregnancy, because we already had plans to meet up at the Sundance Film Festival with a group of my friends. The situation could not have been less ideal. We were crammed into a condo with twelve other people with no privacy and no quiet. One night, I broke down in our room because I was so terrified, scared of whether I could be a mom, of how much work it would be, of what a life change it would be, of losing my freedom. What if I didn't bond with the baby? I hadn't been around many babies at all. What if the child had special needs and I was by myself? What if I had postpartum depression? All of these things were swirling in my head and overwhelming me. The next morning, getting into the shower, I had my only bout of morning sickness. I didn't throw up; I just felt faint and had to lie down on the bathroom floor. I never had another incident of morning sickness. I took it as a sign that the baby was telling me he or she wouldn't be any trouble. I chose to see it as a message, a message that I needed to hear: "It's OK, Mom. We'll make this work."

John and I retreated to a hotel for a night, away from the crowd, and that's where John had *his* freak-out. He was in a complete panic about the situation. John is a bit of a lone wolf. He doesn't travel in a pack of friends like I do. Would he be able to have a connection with a child? He didn't say this, but I was wondering if that was on his mind. We dubbed the night of John's freak-out the Skullcrack, because he was in such a wild panic. He and I were realizing how little we really knew each other. He lived on the other side of the country. That night, I had to talk him down off the ledge, as he had done for me the night before. This was like a romantic comedy, except we were failing to see any comedy in it.

After Sundance, we went on to San Francisco, where I was participating in Sketchfest. We had more heavy times in a hotel room there. In an effort to get my mind off things and provide an escape from the serious conversations, John surprised me with tickets to a dog show that was taking place in a big arena in San Francisco. When I asked what made him get tickets to a dog show, he said, "Well, I know dogs make you happy." How sweet, right? Little did we know the dog show we were going to weren't no Westminster. I think it was some sort of preliminary round to get to the big time. We walked in and found it was held in this superdepressing arena that had rooms but looked like a warehouse. Unkempt people who looked as if they'd been living "off the grid" sat in canvas folding chairs surrounded by dog paraphernalia. Bumper stickers and old signs hung everywhere saying I HEART MY WESTIE or CAUTION—WIGGLEBUTT ZONE! and MY NEWFIE IS SMARTER THAN OUR PRESIDENT! Larger breeds like mastiffs and Saint Bernards were splayed out on the floor, eyes rolling up as if to say, "Get me the hell out of this stank hole." A poodle with its fur in several hair ties and topknots walked endlessly in a circle, obviously insane. We got out of there after about an hour. The energy in the low-rent dog show was even heavier than the energy of a semi-couple discussing an unexpected pregnancy.

We didn't even know what "we" were. We didn't know before this surprise and we hadn't been too concerned about it and we sure didn't know now. We both went back to our separate coasts, uncertain about what our future held. But I did know that if all went well medically, I was having a baby in

September, eight months away, with or without John. I might be a single mom. This was truly bizarre—I was a good girl from the suburbs!

Speaking of which, I decided to tell my parents earlier than the three-month window some people wait for to make sure the baby's OK. I figured I could use the extra support under my unexpected circumstances. There were no grandchildren in our family. My parents weren't the type to say, "Sooo, when are we going to have a grandchild?" and put all that pressure on me, I think because they knew that if I could have been married with kids, I would have pulled it off by now.

I felt bad over the years that my parents weren't going to be grandparents, mainly because I thought they would be really good at it and that it would bring them a lot of joy. Now, I was about to give them some of the best news of their lives. At least, that's what I thought.

I went home for the weekend with the express purpose of telling them the news in person. I even brought the first ultrasound photo of a tiny little tadpole to show them as well. I was nervous all weekend long. Finally, on Sunday morning, I approached them in the living room. "I have some crazy news to tell you," I said. "Um, it's not bad or anything."

In spite of my warning that it wasn't bad, they both got serious looks on their faces.

"Um . . . I'm pregnant."

I thought I was going to be met with a rousing cry of jubilation and excitement. Sure, they hadn't met John, but they were going to be grandparents! Who cares the circumstances? Grandparents! By any means necessary!

Instead, their faces were a collage of "Bleep blop blorp— Does not compute! Does not compute!" And what was that look on my dad's face? It resembled the same grimly set jaw I had seen when I was a teenager and I accidentally hit his Toyota Corolla in the driveway with the other family car. He had the gravity of a doctor, which he is, and I think he mentioned the risks involved with having a baby after forty. What if the baby wasn't healthy? And even if the baby was healthy, they seemed to be thinking, Can our Rachel handle this on her own? My mom said something like, "Are you sure about this? I mean, this isn't like the dog that you can hand back over!"

I'm sure she would say she was making a joke out of nervousness, but I think part of her was truly afraid I might show up at their doorstep and hand the baby off to them, Maury Povich–style, saying, "Sorry, guys, but I gots ta party."

She did get up and hug me, and I *think* she looked happy. She got a little teary even. About a month later, she would send me a bunch of maternity clothes from T.J.Maxx, confirming their support and also reminding me that having a baby to bargain-shop for might be my mother's greatest joy. But at the time, though they said they would support me, I left there that day feeling like Juno. A forty-three-year-old Juno.

After I told good friends and the parents I was pregnant, I then entered the phase where I had to tell people I didn't know as well. This was not quite as fun. People would assume I was trying to get pregnant or they'd ask, "Were you using birth control?" (Yes, they did get that personal.) The answer is, I was not trying to get pregnant and I was using what I thought would be fine for birth control given the onslaught of "It'll never happen" news that had already taken over my brain. I can tell you this: You know those warnings they give you in junior high school health class about how the withdrawal method is not a reliable method of contraception and can still result in pregnancy? Well, now I know firsthand, they weren't just whistlin' Dixie. They meant it!

During what I thought of as my fertile years, I was conscientious, never being careless about birth control whatsoever. But I was pushing forty-four by the time John and I got together. In addition, John's last relationship had been with a woman my age, so he was already quite versed in the over-forty fertility realities. I have several dear friends of similar age who were married and trying to conceive and were having to rely on medical intervention: Clomid or IVF. And I had been told by my doctor that early menopause is often hereditary and could negatively affect my fertility.

With all of these elements, why would I think I could ever get pregnant, especially with my high school birth control methods thrown in for good measure? Look at it this way: If you were ever advising someone on how to get pregnant, would you ever say, "Wait until you are two months shy of your forty-fourth birthday, don't pay any attention to your cycle and the forty-eight hours when you could become pregnant, and, shall we say, withdraw before completing the act? Good luck!"?

I was astounded by what happened. It changed my way of

thinking, because I had fully bought into my own negative future about having a child. No one could have budged me on that. I found the most receptive audience to my story were the single women in their late thirties and early forties, like me, who were used to hearing that motherhood at their age was a difficult if not impossible feat. I was a tiny beacon of hope (or in my case, a bacon of hope) for any one of them who thought they still might want children at some point—one real story to go against the barrage of news reports, magazine articles, advice, and sob stories to the contrary. I knew better than anyone that not everyone is lucky enough to find love during their "safety" years and that not every woman is cut out to say, "Whatever. I'm doing it alone."

As opposed to the awe I was eliciting from the single ladies, I noticed a vastly different response when I told women my age with kids who'd been married for many years. "Were you using birth control?" When I'd tell them the honest answer, they would laugh at me! They downright scolded me as if I were a teenager! "Rachel! That's HIGH SCHOOL stuff!" a woman whom I do not know well enough to have been sharing my personal information said to me. To which I could have replied, "Oh yeah?! Well, I wasn't having sex in high school!" I always got a bit angry when I heard this "duh" reaction, because of course a married woman who had her kids *right on schedule* has never really taken in and *felt* the barrage of "YOU BETTER HAVE KIDS BEFORE FORTTYYYYYY OR YOU MAY HAVE FERTILITY ISSUUUUUES!" news stories and magazine articles and general conversations that a single woman who may still want kids hears and pays attention to and has to contend with on a regular basis. Also, I always thought all the warnings they give to teens about not relying on the withdrawal method was just some bullshit you told high school kids who had no control of their bodies. I honestly didn't think people really got pregnant that way. Yes, I did purport earlier that I was in the "smart" classes.

I've Got Spirit!

•—•

During the pregnancy, I felt quite sure the baby would make it to full term. The disadvantage of being of "advanced maternal age" is that you do have a higher chance of miscarriage. However, I felt I would be having this baby, because I realized I had been told just that by Shelley the Channeler not quite one year ago.

I know that reading all these stories about pigs and dreams and The Secret might make the reader think I am super-into the metaphysical and really New Age-y. I'm definitely open to that stuff, but I don't think of myself as airy-fairy. I feel more like I started to notice the strange phenomena around me rather than be closed off to them. This whole ball got rolling in a sense when my friend Josan took me to see Shelley the Channeler on my birthday a few months before I met John. Josan herself is psychic—not for a living, not for money, but it's just a gift she has. So that year on my birthday, I was in LA, and Josan picked me up for a birthday lunch and told me after-

ward, "We are going to see my friend Shelley the Channeler."
"OK," I said, "bring it on!"

We arrived at her house in Rancho Palos Verdes and I met
Shelley—a woman of about sixty with a slight Midwestern
twang. Or, I don't know, maybe she was a lifelong mellow Cali-
fornian. But she didn't greet us drenched in crystals or dream-
catchers or anything like that.

Shelley channels a spirit named Kendra. So you sit on her
couch and she does this sort of blessing thing and then her
head pops up and she has become Kendra. Kendra speaks with
an accent akin to an Indian accent and her eyes are bright and
girlish and her voice is chirpy like a bird's.

"Hello! How are you?"

I couldn't help but giggle a bit self-consciously.

"Um. I'm fine."

"Good!" says Kendra. "I'm very glad you are here to see
me!"

Kendra starts talking to me about who I am, who my family is to me, what I worry about, what my strengths are, and it
was all spot-on. Instantly. It wasn't the kind of stuff you could
find through Google. It was like she knew my emotions, my
concerns, anxieties, not facts and external things about me.
She wouldn't say, "Now, do you have a brother?" trying to feel
out my situation. She would definitively say, "Your brother is
experiencing this or that." So I'm already instantly impressed.

Also, side story here—I had done a visioning workshop
once in California. OK, now it's really hard to believe I'm not
into all this stuff, but just go with me here. We were supposed
to imagine our spirit guide taking us on a journey. Everyone in

the workshop seemed to be able to imagine a spirit guide, a specific person they had never met, with a face they could see, that would lead them on this journey. Try as I might, I could not envision a spirit guide. Every time the leader mentioned the guide, I had to confess to myself that this vision just wasn't happening for me. Instead, I kept envisioning a blue dot. About the height of a person, my spirit guide looked not unlike a large, blue, iridescent M&M. But I referred to it as the Blue Dot—not the Blue Circle or the Blue Orb—the Blue Dot. I would joke with the other participants during the breaks, because I had shared with a few of them that I couldn't see a person, so every time the leader would say, "Your spirit guide takes you by the hand" or "Your spirit guide takes you into their arms," I'd think, "My guide doesn't have arms! It's just a blue M&M!"

This workshop had taken place several years ago. I hadn't thought of it or the Blue Dot in a long time. As I was sitting on the couch and listening to Kendra the Spirit talking to me, she said, "You are guided by the spirit of the Blue Dot."

In the tradition of the Great Writers who have gone before me, I will now call upon the phrase "I shit you not."

Kendra did make a few predictions for me. She said, "You are going to meet a man in three months. No, wait, six months—in three to six months."

By now, I hadn't dated anyone seriously for five years, so this seemed too good to be true.

"What should I do to meet him?" I asked. I was thinking, "Does this mean I have to go on Match.com?"

"You won't have to *do* anything. Also, you are going to have one child."

I was highly skeptical of this prediction. Sure, that would be lovely if it were true. I would like to believe. But did this spirit from India or somewhere that had an accent that sounded mildly Indian realize that I was turning forty-three at the time and I was completely single? Having a child would mean defying some major odds. It would have to be some sort of miracle at this point. Nevertheless, I didn't want to offend Kendra. I nodded politely.

Four months later, I met John in the bar. I didn't have to *do* anything. He just started talking to me. And a little less than a year after Kendra told me, I learned I would be having a baby. The whole time in that iffy stage of the first trimester, even when I was thinking, "Well, you never know, this might not 'take' due to my age and the chance of miscarriage," Kendra's words were in the back of my head. I didn't even tell John about Kendra, but I had a feeling of "Oh, this is going to happen," because Kendra the Vaguely Indian Spirit had told me I was going to have one child.

What to Expect When You're Not Expecting

●—●

I open the book What to Expect When You're Expecting, sent to me by a dear friend from home. The first line is "So you've made the decision to start a family. . . ." In my mind, that sentence became "So you've made the highly premeditated decision to start a family. You and your HUSBAND have been planning and anticipating this for years. It's finally time! The glorious miracle of life is within you, and you are aglow with excitement and anticipation." My brain goes blank. Where's the book that starts out "So you're forty-three and think you can't have kids but unexpectedly got pregnant on a trip to Hawaii with a guy you've known for six months who you think is a good guy but the two of you aren't even close to any sort of commitment?" Where is *that* book?

After San Francisco, John showed signs that he would be supportive in some fashion, though I didn't know to what extent. I remember he sent me a big gift certificate for maternity clothes that made me feel like he wasn't going to run away or not show up. I think that made my parents think he was a good guy as well. They still had yet to meet him. He ended up visiting me about once a month or so and was helping me out when he was here, but because he lived in California, I went to most all of my doctor's appointments solo. I honestly didn't mind, though. I had many friends offer to accompany me, especially to the amnio appointment, but I declined. I like braving the doctor's by myself, and if I have someone there with a concerned look on their face, saying, "Are you okaaay?" it can take me out of my strong zone. I did have my friend David, one of the Dartmouth Gays, accompany me to the genetic counseling session, because I wanted a second person there to think up questions I might have forgotten and to help me remember everything after it was over. I went ahead with the amnio, and everything—all those "advanced maternal age" problems the doctors look for—checked out OK.

I tried checking one of those week-by-week pregnancy Web sites. Here's what it said:

YOUR PREGNANCY: WEEK 22

If your list of baby things to do seems to be getting longer the bigger you get, don't stress out. Make a pact with your partner that one day or evening a week, you'll do something that has nothing to do with the baby. How about the latest Anne Hathaway flick and dinner?

What if my partner lives in California and is just trying to do the right thing by preparing to be a good dad and we don't quite know yet where we stand with each other and he isn't here to take me to the latest damn Anne Hathaway flick? Or worse yet, what if I were a woman whose partner had skipped out and wanted nothing to do with his child and so that "list of baby things to do that's getting longer" can't be sweetened by a partner one evening a week or any evening ever? Because there are women out there who are reading that Web site who are in that situation, and ain't no Anne Hathaway flick gonna solve that.

I was feeling scared. Anne Hathaway wasn't going to help.

Giggles and Tears

●–●

Now I *was the one* who was pregnant and *I* was about
to be the perpetrator of my very own shower on innocent vic-
tims. I hoped to make it as painless as possible. My shower
would be coed and in the evening, so I hoped it would feel just
like a regular gathering with only a small time allotted to look
at tiny pants.

I didn't know the first thing about what a baby needs or
what items would be necessary to make my life infinitely easier, but I had to create a registry. So I brought in the experts:
David and Russell. Maybe because they felt lucky to have won
the adoption lottery, or maybe because they actually had to
pass the test of being "worthy" of being good parents (unlike
the rest of us), but whatever the case, they had done more
research on infant care and more preparation before they
became fathers than any other parents I knew.

At the insistence of David, we did not meet at the Babies "R"
Us right near my apartment but rather on the Upper West Side
at a store called Giggle. This is high-end, gay-worthy baby stuff

we are talking. I had just seen the documentary *Babies*, which features the lives of happy babies in Africa and Mongolia, so absolutely all of the store items were looking particularly unnecessary right now to me anyway, and I just wanted to register for some sticks, a few goats, and a swarm of flies to create a truly happy and adorable child.

The second I walked into Giggle, I started to feel a ball of anxiety taking over my body. I could see it appearing on the horizon, getting larger and larger, but I was trying to wait to acknowledge it until the process was over. The anxiety was "Oh my God! I could be doing this alone." My sunshiny outlook, which I had carefully fed and cultivated for five months, was faltering at the sight of the brightly colored Happy Town I was entering. Each toy with googly eyes seemed to stare me down with a challenging expression: "Aren't you happy? Aren't we cute? This is the moment you've been waiting for. IS THERE ANYTHING BETTER THAN THIS?"

We started off in the stroller area. "Do you want me to walk you through how this works?" asked the clerk. Aaaand . . . Brain Shutdown. White TV Fuzz. I knew I would not absorb one thing she said, let alone remember it four months later when the baby finally arrived. I was too busy fighting the fear. "No, let's save that to the end," I said. We moved on to the next department, the Breast Area.

"Oh, Lord. No, no, cannot compute, no, no, no." I could not handle learning about the mysteries of breast-feeding right away. Yes, I planned on breast-feeding, but all I could think was "Not now. Please, not now." I had recently seen Maya Rudolph at our *SNL* reunion show and she was pumping breast milk in an office. I had never seen this before. Believe me, it looked like a damn horror show. I didn't know nipples could stretch that far. "Um, can we save Breast Town for later too?" This was only the second department we had approached and the second thing I was asking to save for later. I knew that whatever department came next, I would have to face it. It's like if you taste wine at a restaurant and it's really bad so you ask to try another wine, but then the thing is, you have to like that second one or you are just being a pain in the ass. Sometimes the second one is even worse, and I'll choke out through a grimace, "That's great. Yes, that one." Notice how I'm turning to a wine analogy for a baby store. Is that a bad sign? Well, it's what I knew. I knew wine. I did not know nipples.

We moved on to the cribs. I could handle cribs. I peered into a high-end crib that had cute padding around all the sides. "Now," said David, "some people are against this padding that goes around the sides, because the baby can roll over and get their face pressed up against it and they can . . ." He trailed off and made a face of "and you know what happens next." I filled in the blank for him. "She dead."

He nodded and continued, "But if you take the padding off of the crib, they can hit their heads on the bars." OK. So this crib poses the question: With which method do you want to kill your baby?

From here on in, each item came with a cautionary tale from David about how each thing you "had to have" could easily turn into a death trap if you weren't very clear on the instructions. Car seat? "If you put them in the car seat," said David, "make sure to not just buckle the strap that goes across their chest. You also have to fasten the strap that comes up between their legs. Some people don't do the strap between the legs and then the baby can slide downward and . . ."

I filled in the blank for him. "And . . . she dead."

Baby slings? I had just read about a recall of certain baby slings. You don't get the right kind . . . she dead. You had to know the instructions. Side note: I never read instructions. Not on my BlackBerry, not on my camera. I am probably missing out on hundreds of functions just because I shut down when reading instructions. So I don't know how to use the zoom function on my camera. But it's not going to *kill a baby*!

We moved on to the socks section. I breathed a sigh of relief. "Ahhhhh! I know socks. I can handle socks." I even doubled back to Breast Town, feeling I could finally tackle it. I had waded around in the pool and was ready for the deep end.

I left the store feeling accomplished. I had done it. I had registered. There was so much more to do, but I had gotten over the first hurdle. I said good-bye to David and Russell and thanked them profusely. I was going to meet my friend Ricki to see a play, and as I started to walk, I had the nagging, tugging feeling that I was going to cry. Not tears of joy. Not tears of "You did it! Good for you. What a big step!" Tears of straight-up fear. I *was* alone. I could be handling all these things alone. I didn't know if I was up for the challenge. I felt a complete lack of confidence expand and take over. I didn't cry, though. I got on the subway and met Ricki. We sat in our seats in the theater and waited for the lights to go down.

"How'd it go with David and Russell?"

"Good," I said. "They were really helpful. But I feel like . . ."

"What?"

"I feel like I might cry."

And then I did. Sitting in the seat, surrounded by other theatergoers, I felt tears start to form in my eyes and run down my face.

"Ohhh," said Ricki, a mother of three kids with a fantastically helpful and involved husband. "It'll be OK."

Something deep within was telling me it would be OK, but for now this was Fear Day, and I guess I just had to let it happen. This stuff had to come out at some point, I suppose. It's weird that it happened at a place called Giggle.

A few months later, Ricki ended up throwing me my version of the perfect shower: It was at night, it was coed, alcohol was served, and to spare others the pain of all those hours I had logged over the years, I raced through the gifts in record speed.

I have a confession, though. I did receive some baby jeans from the Gap. In spite of my previous convictions, upon opening them, I did say, "Awwww!" and got a little teary over the cuteness of those tiny pants.

We Are Thrilled to Announce the Birth of... Hercules!?

●–●

Three months into the pregnancy and I was sure it was a girl. I have always been right in guessing the genders of my friends' kids in the womb, and the second I found out I was pregnant, I just knew it was a girl. I was thinking only about girl names, so sure was I. I did want to find out the gender ahead of time because I already had enough uncertainty about so many aspects of the whole process, though to me, with my self-proclaimed psychic powers, this was just a formality. I went in for an ultrasound one day and the nurse said, "Do you want to know the sex of your baby?"

"Yes," I said.

"It's a boy!"

All the springs in my head went *boioioioioioioioingnngngngg*. The nurse kept talking, but my brain was just a blur. I had this girl vision comfortably settled in my head and now that had been turned upside down. I realized as I was absorbing the news that maybe I had made this baby a girl in my mind to make myself feel more at ease. I'm a girl. I *know* girls. I know what they like to do, and if it was just going to be me as a single mom, I could picture that. Something about having a boy and possibly not having his dad around made me more nervous, even though that may have been an irrational thought. I called up John to tell him the news. He seemed freaked out too, like he may be having the same irrational thought.

At some point in all of the proceedings, I think when I was about six months along, though I never outright requested it of him, John told me he was planning on moving to New York. He said he couldn't imagine going through his day in California, knowing he had a child growing up across the country. Luckily, with his job, he could work from anywhere. Again, we still hadn't figured *us* out, but I was imagining having to explain to my child why his dad wasn't here when many of the other kids' dads were, so I was relieved to know that my baby would have his dad in his life. I'm still going to have explaining to do since I don't know that we will be a conventional family, but luckily, I live in New York City at the moment, capital of the unconventional families. For now, the plan was that John would find an apartment near me and sublet his place in California. There were the basic logistics of space concerns with my one-bedroom apartment and John working out of his home, but also, given the short amount of time we had dated, we both just felt more comfortable playing it safe. Yes, putting us all in the same tiny apartment would work for the romantic comedy version of the story, but as we already learned in chapter one, I ain't a leading lady in a rom-com.

Since this baby was now officially our mutual concern, we could bring up the topic of names. For boys, I loved all the Old Testament names. I made up a list with names like Caleb and Levi. I even threw in some more odd ones, one of my favorite odd ones being Zebediah, because I thought Zeb sounded cool. John liked the traditional name of Jack. He also liked Hayden. When he said that name, I burst out laughing in spite of myself. "What's so funny?" he said. I couldn't stop laughing, mainly because Hayden is exactly the name I would think he would pick—so him and so un-me. We were still tossing around the same few names we had managed to agree on a few months later. One day, I texted him simply "Zebediah? Just keeping it in the mix!"

He texted back: "In the mix? Try putting it in the blender."

Just a few months into the pregnancy, I had a dream about a little boy named Hercules. When I woke up, I called John and told him. We chuckled about it, and I began referring to the creature within as Hercules. It soon lost its comic-book, jokey image as a name and actually started to sound really cool to me. "How's Herc doing?" John would call up and ask. I started to really like the name Hercules. Like for real. There were a few problems with the name, though. One: If I told my mom I was naming the baby Hercules, her head would fall off. Two: Every time I would tell someone his name, I don't think I could face the derision and "WHAT?! HERCULES?" that would come my way. I don't have the strength to weather that every day. Also, in my dream, Hercules was saying that his father wouldn't hug him or kiss him—he seemed sad: my not-so-subconscious concerns about raising a child whose father might not live in the same town and—at the time I had the dream—whose future level of involvement was a complete unknown. Oh, and finally, if I had any job other than actor, Hercules might actually fly. But people would think I was just picking a weird name because I'm a crazy actor instead of that I had the dream. (Add Hercules to Banjo, Pilot Inspektor, Kal-El—we all see *US* magazine.) In spite of these strikes against the name Hercules, we still called the baby Herc right up 'til the end. One day we were walking in the West Village and saw a business plaque on the side of the building: HERCULES KOSTAS, CPA. "Look!" we exclaimed. "Someone actually named Hercules!" See? It can be a real name! Yes, this man was probably Greek, but so what? we chuckled. The next day, we were watching the World Cup. We noticed a player on the US team was named Herculez (with a z) Gomez. "What!? Another Hercules? It's a sign!" we thought. "OK," we said, "if we see one more sign of Hercules in the next twenty-four hours, that's the Universe telling us we are supposed to name the baby Hercules." That night, we went to Shakespeare in the Park and saw *The Merchant of Venice*. Out of nowhere, one of the characters looks skyward and cries out to the heavens and ye gods on high, "Go, Hercules!" John and I whipped our heads toward each other, wide-eyed, and chuckled to ourselves in disbelief as the play continued. Even when the baby was a few days old, I still thought of him as Herc, but I ended up letting go of the name. I have a hard enough time fending off the negative input that can come your way when you put yourself out there to be an actor. I didn't need the added unwanted input every time I told someone my baby's name.

"Oh, what a cute baby! What's his name?"

"Um, it's . . . Hercules."

"WHAT!? Hercules?! What kind of name is *that*? *Hercules*?"

No. I didn't have the strength. Plus, I must reemphasize, my mother's head would fall off.

How to Care for Your F'in' Baby

•—•

I hadn't been around many babies at all. Neither had John. In fact, we had no idea what the hell we were doing, but we were hoping instinct and helpful friends and family would get us through. For some peace of mind, we signed up for a class on infant care, a private session with a teacher who came to my apartment. I had to do *something* to feel like I was preparing to have this baby. I didn't even glance at a birthing book until I was about seven months pregnant. I had previously thought I was escaping this one excruciating hallmark of womanhood, and now that I was having a baby, I just stuck my head in the ground and sang, "La la la la!" I took the approach of "Well, it's gotta get out somehow!" Since I was doing no preparation about the birth, I felt I should do something to make me feel prepared in some capacity. Hence the class. Meredith, the teacher, showed up, a cool-looking slightly crunchy lady—she fit the image I had of someone who would teach such a class—and she started to teach us about infant care.

First lesson: "There's no sense in trying to build a schedule for an infant. For the first three months, there is no sleep scheduling to be done. You just let them sleep when they want." This was the best advice that she gave us, actually. I didn't know about that. "You don't let them 'cry it out' when they are so young. They are crying because they need something. Now, later, when they're a little older and crying, you might be like, 'Fuck it,' and let them cry it out."

Was that . . . ? Did I just hear . . . ? The F-word? Oh jeez. I think I did. I could feel John withdraw his faith in this woman the instant she dropped it. It didn't bother me, but John isn't a big fan of swearing, especially in a professional situation.

"When you're swaddling, you want to wrap it from one side, then the bottom, and tuck that in over here, and then wrap the other side like this. Sometimes people think they have to be delicate with babies, but they are soothed by being held really tightly, so you can get a really snug fit and just really fuckin' wrap them tight."

No. OK. Definitely heard that one. Lady, please. You have a Midwesterner here, from the real world, not the New York artsy world, and I want him to pay attention and have his first words after you leave the room be "I feel much better prepared to be a father!" not "Did you hear how many F-Bombs she dropped?"

"When the baby first starts pooping, it will have what's called meconium. It's a dark, tarry stool. The first time you see it, you may be like, 'What the fuck is that?' "

Out of the corner of my eye, I saw John's jaw twitch ever so slightly. OK, I'm not going to take responsibility for this woman. I'm going to let it go . . . just let it go. . . .

She proceeded to drop five more before the session was through, clocking in at a grand total of eight. Lest you think I exaggerate, I assure you, John was counting. As soon as she left, sure enough, John said, "She dropped eight F-Bombs."

I think if I'd been alone, I certainly would have registered that it's an odd profession to be tossing around the F-word. It wouldn't bother me, though. I just would have reported it to friends later as a funny story. It would be hard to be in comedy and take offense at the F-word. That's tame talk in comedy circles. I couldn't say John didn't have a point, though. I could see using the F-word a lot if you were teaching lessons on "How to Do Heroin" or "Graffiti 101" or even how to play the electric guitar— something badass. But it was a bit of a mismatch for infant care.

Once I had the baby, I realized that the class was pretty unnecessary, since everything she taught us the nurses teach you in the hospital. Except that thing about when they are less than three months old, you don't have to schedule them at all, which was a helpful fact. In hindsight, the whole thing was a bit of a waste, except that it made me feel I was putting in the prep time so junior wouldn't know he was born to a complete novice.

Yet still, I suppose in a sense that Meredith's advice stayed with me. Once our baby was born, every time I fed him or put him down for a nap, every time I changed a diaper or swaddled him, I remembered that caring for a baby is the most sacred fuckin' event of your entire fuckin' life.

A Letter from
the Prophet Doug

●–●

John would visit from Mill Valley about once a month
during the pregnancy. He was always sweet and attentive, going
to Whole Foods to get mangoes and watermelon—my two crav-
ings. Whenever I would wonder what the hell was going to happen to us as a couple, I didn't focus on it all that much, like I
would have as a single lady trying to figure out her relationship,
because the pregnancy and the planning were where all my
energy was going. The crazy thing was, I hadn't even met John's
family and wasn't going to meet his parents until after the
birth. One day, I got an e-mail forwarded to me from John. It
was from John's younger brother, Doug.

Rachel,
This note is long overdue. I should have written it a
few months ago after getting the good news from
John, but you know it's hard (or at least a little bit

awkward) to reach out to a stranger. The big problem is figuring out what to say or really just how to get started.

Turns out it is really not that complicated. It is a simple matter of starting off with a "congratulations!" and a sincere: "Welcome to the family."

I am truly very excited about the arrival of this little boy.

You know for a long time, I guess my entire life, I've looked up to my brother, as younger brothers always do. As a child I was jealous of his athletic talent and his dancing ability (there was a time when he thought he was Prince). As an adult I envied his jet-set lifestyle and a passport that took him around the world. But nearly six years ago, when my own son was born, I thought I had reached a point when things had leveled off. At that time, it just appeared that fatherhood was something that may not be in the cards for my older brother.

That would have been a shame. I know there are deadbeat dads, baby's daddies, and those who see fatherhood as only sending a check once a month. And there are guys like John. I am sure he is nervous right now, wondering what kind of father he'll be—but that is the exact thing a good dad does at this stage. Truth is he's a lock. He was meant to play this role. I know that from the devotion he has always had for his family, and I know that

especially firsthand from the help he showed me
this year in waging a fight for my own son.

Fatherhood will change John. It will probably
slow him down a step or two, soften him up a bit
and bring out a goofy side that causes him to make
strange faces or sing nursery rhymes or do anything
he can to bring out a smile and giggle from a little
boy who's captured his heart.

Rachel, I am sure your friends have told you to
get ready, that there is nothing like the
unconditional love a mother has for her child.
They're right. That bond is instant. But what you
and John will discover is, the truly amazing part is
not the love you will give but the vast amount that
flows from a child to his parents. There is no way to
prepare for it. It will happen within the first day or
so. The baby will cry and you'll wonder if he's
hungry or needs a diaper change, and then you'll
pick him up and he'll instantly stop. Everything was
okay, he just wanted to be held. In that moment
nothing else, including the old ways we use to define
ourselves, any longer matters: What you weigh,
where's your hairline (that one's more of a guy
issue), how much is in the bank account, where you
went to college or what you achieved in your career
is all irrelevant to this little child. All that matters
to him is that you're his parent, that you're his
mommy and daddy, and that is more than enough
for him.

I guess that is why this is a letter of congratulations. Not because you're about to have a baby, but because you are about to feel an unconditional love like you've never been exposed to before. I am truly excited for both you and John. I look forward to meeting you some day soon, and especially look forward to meeting this little guy.

So welcome to the family! You've given us reason to celebrate two additions.

Doug

I read this letter on an Amtrak train, and I don't think of myself as an Ol' Softy, but I had tears streaming down my face when I finished it. It could have been the hormones, I guess. I called up John and said, "Oh my God, I'm crying from this letter!" He revealed that it had made him cry as well. Then I sent it to my mom and a friend from home, not mentioning my tears, just saying how nice it was. They both called me back crying. Uncle Doug had created a trail of tears up the Eastern Seaboard.

Because of all his wisdom, we dubbed him the Prophet Doug. Later, when our baby would be crying and we didn't know why, and we would just pick him up to hold him, that became known as the Prophet Doug move. Then it became just a casual verb on its own. The baby would be crying, and one of us would say, "Does his diaper need changing? Did he eat? Did you try Prophet Douging him?"

Besides the fact that Doug became a verb, I'm including

his letter because, though this is my story, I'm telling John's story as well, and I thought you should know that beneath all of my quips or observations, some of which John may feel more comfortable keeping private, and whether or not we are together as a couple or as co-parents, the fact is, this guy did uproot his life from a quiet hamlet across the whole country to a busy loud avenue in New York City so that he could be a daily part of his son's life. I thought he deserved some credit for that. Not everyone would do that. And I thought Prophet Doug said it better than I ever could.

With All Due Respect to Edgar Allan Poe

•—•

In spite of the fact that I'm not a megastar, occasional perks come along for me because I was at one time on *Saturday Night Live*. Nothing major. Stuff like an open table at a busy restaurant. I lucked out big-time, though, when I was five months pregnant. I was walking down the street and a guy said, "Hi! I produced your segment on Tony Danza's show a few years ago." Not to say I may have blocked out my guest stint on the esteemed yet short-lived Tony Danza talk show, but I didn't remember this guy. To be friendly, however, I talked to him for a bit and asked what he was doing now, to which he responded that he was working for the Nate Berkus show. Nate Berkus was Oprah's design guy; he did all of her home makeovers for the show, and all of Oprah's audience was completely in love with him because he is so attractive and sweet and talented that they all just blocked out the tiny fact that he is gay. It's kind of a Don't Ask, Don't Tell policy that the fans made with themselves so they could still fantasize that someday he will do over their home *and* have romantic and caring sex with them.

This guy Paul asked if I needed a room done for my apartment. At first I was about to say no and then I realized, "Wait a minute! Yes! I have to somehow create a nursery in my bedroom since I live in a one-bedroom apartment and I'm having a baby." Paul said he'd run it by the producers, and to my delight, I got a call a few weeks later that they were into the idea of doing my room! *I* get to have a room designed by Nate Berkus?! I felt like I had won some Oprah sweepstakes.

They came over and filmed the whole "before" segment, and Nate was just as charming in person as he is on TV, and incidentally, the room he came up with is great. He split my bedroom between my area and the baby's area with a partition, and somehow it really feels like two separate rooms. Everything went off without a hitch. Well, that is, except for the Telltale Dildo.

Please. Please. Let me explain. I need to give you some background information. This may come as a shock to you, but if I may use *Sex and the City* terms, I am not a Samantha. I'm probably more of a Charlotte. At this point in life, I'm not interested in random sex with some stranger or a one-night stand. I'm not exactly looking for Mr. Goodbar. In my spare time, I'm not buying garter belts or Chinese sex swings, and I've never set foot in a sex-toy shop and I think I would die of mortification to do so. You know who wouldn't die of mortification to do so, though? A sex addict—Addict Three. I need to specify here that when dating Addict Three, I had no idea of his addiction, because dating a sex addict is not all it's cracked up to be. The thing about a sex addict is, they are usually not addicted to sex with *you*. At least, as my luck would have it, that was my particular situation. Since I didn't find out about his addiction until we had broken up, it's not something we were *dealing* with, having long talks about, or trying to solve *together* as a couple. He revealed it to me afterward, so I really am not sure what manifestation it took—Porn? Hos? Watching someone in high heels eat fried chicken? I have no idea. It was no longer my concern. This is all background to tell you that he did buy me a sex toy . . . a bright red vibrator. No pun intended, but as it turned out, it really wasn't my thing.

There it sat in my top dresser drawer, unused for years. I forgot all about it. Occasionally, I'd think, "I really should throw away that bright red dildo," usually when I was boarding a plane and imagining it going down and my parents coming to deal with my apartment. "Oh, look, Paul, here are all the old photos. And here are her reviews from over the years. And here . . . Oh! My word!"

So I would think, I really should throw that away. Living in an apartment in New York City, the thought of disposing of a bright red dildo really just makes you go "meh" and leave it for another day. You can't just drop it down the garbage chute. Well, you could, I guess. For my peace of mind, I'd have to properly dispose of it, making sure there were no identifying pieces of mail in the bag. That's just me. So there it sat, alone in the top drawer of my dresser, hidden behind some belts and some bathing suits.

When the Nate Berkus staff came to redo my room, at some point during the day, I thought of that bright red dildo. "Aw, I

really should have moved that, I guess. To a place they definitely wouldn't be stumbling across it." But then I thought,
"That's silly. Why would they ever be going through my draw-
ers to redo my room?" They were going to be painting, putting
up a partition, moving some stuff around. Everything would
be fine. I smiled—for what had I to fear?

Still, as the day went on, that vibrator transformed into the
Telltale Dildo. I could almost hear it buzzing from time to time.

"I should have moved it." "*Bzzzz BZZZZ! Bzzzz BZZZZ*," it
sounded in my imagination. "Why didn't I deal with that years
ago?" "*Bzzzz BZZZZ! Bzzzz BZZZZ!*" It grew louder and louder
with each passing hour.

"What would have been so difficult about throwing away
that bright red dildo, Rachel?" "*Bzzzz BZZZZ BZZZZ
B Z Z Z Z Z Z Z Z Z Z Z Z Z Z Z Z Z Z Z Z Z Z !
BZZZZZZZZZZZZZZZZZZZZZZZZ!*"

"OK. Knock it off, Dratch. You're being ridiculous. No,
you're being ridickulous. Ha! That's—"

"Excuse me, Rachel?" said the producer for the segment,
poking her head out of my bedroom.

"Yeah?"

"We're putting up the partition and they were wondering
if, to make it secure, they can drill a hole through your dresser
to attach it to the partition."

"Oh, sure."

"OK, so they'll just have to drill one hole, so they're just
going to need to remove the top drawer."

"*B Z Z Z Z Z Z Z Z Z Z Z Z Z Z Z Z Z Z Z Z Z Z Z Z !
BZZZZZZZZZZZZZZZZ! BZZZZZZZZZZZZZZZZZZ!*"

I *wish* I were making this up.

If I were *using* the thing. If I were one of those girls who was like, "OK! But don't mess up my sex toys! They're all in order! Ha-HAAA! Cackle Cackle Donkey Laugh HAAA!" Fine. But I'm just not that girl! I went into fight-or-flight response. Milling around my room were two Latino workmen, several underlings, and producers, and there was about to be a horrifying reveal of the Telltale Dildo.

Oh God! What COULD I do? BZZZZ BZZZZ. BZZZZ BZZZZ. BZZZZ BZZZZ. Was it possible they heard not? No! No? Almighty God! They heard!—They suspected!—They KNEW!

Fooling *absolutely no one*, I told the producer I needed to get some things out of the drawer. She kindly shooed everyone out of the room while I did some of the worst acting of my life (and that's saying something), pulling decoy items out of the drawer to fill a shopping bag—bras, bathing suits, you know, things you would just *die* if some people saw. . . . What! Underwear!?! Oh no! You would hate for a roomful of people to see that you wore underwear! Cast away your eyes, Latino workmen! For my dainty underthings you shall not see! No. I'm sure everyone in the room, including the Latino workmen, knew I was squirreling away some sort of sex device. Only they probably multiplied the actual item by a drawerful and threw in various shapes and sizes and colors and attachments in their imaginations.

Eventually, I did dispose of the Telltale Dildo, though it sat in my living room for a few weeks in that bag of bathing suits and bras, among all of the baby gifts that had started to pile up. Finally, the fear of a second discovery by my mom or some helpful friend offering to put away all my baby gifts made me put it in a bag and then another bag and drop it down the garbage chute. It's probably lying in a landfill somewhere now. And some say, when the moon is full, you can still hear its angry roar. *Hark! Louder! Louder! LOUDER!! It is the buzzing of the Telltale Dildo!* BZZZZ BZZZZZZZ! BZZZZ BZZZZZZZ! BZZZZ BZZZZZZZZZ!

'Tis 'Mones

•––•

I had the good fortune of being pregnant at the same time as my friend Amy Poehler. Amy had been through pregnancy before, so she was helpful and gave me lots of good advice. She didn't follow all the strict rules about alcohol. She ate sushi, for God's sake. One night, we went to a restaurant. She was more visibly pregnant than I, and the waiter asked if I would like a drink and then turned to Amy and said, "And *you* can't *have* a drink!" To which Amy shot dagger eyes and said pointedly, "*Yes*, I can!" Don't stand between a pregnant lady and her wine.

I didn't have too many problems with hormones. Usually, I felt like I had happy hormones running through me—I took everything in stride in a new way. But if Amy was having a hormone day, she would say, "'Tis 'mones, my friend, 'tis 'mones!"

I did have one incident of 'mones. John and I were at a wedding in Wisconsin. We were sitting at the bar after the rehearsal dinner. Some of the guests were singing karaoke. I was six months pregnant and drinking a seltzer with lime. John had a beer. The familiar strains of the harmonica came on the speaker system—the beginning of the Billy Joel song "Piano Man."

"Oh no! This song makes me sad," I said.

"I love this song! Why does it make you sad?" said John.

"*Why* does it make me sad? Have you listened to the words?"

"Not really," said John.

"You've never listened to the words of 'Piano Man'?!" And I started singing along, staring at him pointedly to emphasize the tragedies he'd been missing out on by not listening closely enough.

"He says, 'Son, can you play me a memory? I'm not really sure how it goes. But it's sad and it's sweet and I knew it complete when I wore a younger man's clooooothes!'"

"OK, OK. So? I still love this song!"

I continued singing along, banging on the bar with my hand for emphasis.

"He says, 'BILL, I beLIEVE this is KILLing me,' as a smile ran away from his face. 'Well, I'm SURE that I COULD be a movie star if I could get out of this place!'" I was looking John right in the eyes and laughing, but at the same time my eyes were filling up with tears, welling up right there in the bar.

John started laughing. "OK! OK!"

"It's sooo sad!!" Next verse. I was not letting up. No siree. *"Now Paul is a real estate novelist, who never had time for a wife. And he's talking with Davy, who's still in the navy, and PROBABLY WILL BE FOR LIFE!"*

"Oh my God! Okaaay! Take it easy!"

At this point, in spite of my laughter, I had tears of melancholy streaming down my face. I was wiping them away with my hand. I grabbed John's wrist with my free hand.

"'SING US A SONG, YOU'RE THE PIANO MAAAAAN! SING US A SONG TONIIIIIGHT! WELL WE'RE ALL IN THE MOOD FOR A MELODYYYYY. AND YOU'VE GOT US FEELING ALL RIIIIIIGHT!'"

Now I had a bar napkin to wipe away my tears, crying and laughing uncontrollably. I was like a hysterical woman out of an old movie who needed to be slapped across the face.

A week later, I heard the song come on the radio again. I texted John—"Guess what song is on right now. 'Piano Man'!"

He texted me back. "I used to like that song 'til some girl ruined it for me."

What can I say? 'Twas 'mones, my friend. 'Twas 'mones.

The Day I Became a "Baby Person"

●—●

The baby was due September 20. About six weeks out from that date, I learned Herc had turned around and was breech, poised to come out feetfirst, which usually means you have to have a C-section. There are homeopathic remedies to get the baby to flip. I'm not sure what was making me all nature girl about this stuff, but I was trying to avoid having a C-section. I went to a chiropractor who specializes in baby flipping. I went to an acupuncturist—a different acupuncturist than the Chinese storefront place, needless to say. (That's "needless," not "needle-less." Ba-dum-bum.) According to the world of acupuncture, one of the ways to get your baby to flip—and this is for real—is to hold up lit incense a few inches from your pinky toes for twenty minutes a night. This is actually some ancient, 2,000-year-old Chinese secret called moxibustion. Something about the heat channeling into that particular meridian can flip your baby. (OK, at this point, I may as well just own that maybe I *am* into the idea of a metaphysical, other-plane, nonscientific world. Damn, as I look back, I've talked about prophetic dreams, channelers, messages from pigs, Blue Dot spirit guides, and now smoking up your toes—maybe I need to reconsider my self-perception.) Anyway, John was along for the ride: The guy who last year at this time was at the San Fran Food and Wine Fest, wearing a Vineyard Vines shirt, now found himself holding incense up for twenty minutes a night to the toes of a Jewess.

By now, Amy Poehler had had her baby, Abel, a week prior, and I went over to see him. There he was, newly born, tiny and frail and birdlike as any week-old baby would be.

"Here, do you want to hold him?"

"Noooo!" I thought. "Yes!" I said.

Mind you, my baby was due right around the corner; I was going to be in charge of one of these baby birds in *five weeks*! What if I let the head flop back? How do I hold the head? The head! The head! The neck. The head! I instantly wanted to toss him out of my hands like I was in a game of Hot Potato, but social decorum and human ethics prevailed. I held him for about two minutes, all the while having what would be my last panic attack on the topic of Whatifisuckasamom? I left Amy's apartment full of anxiety and self-doubt. The topic of panic trended with me for the rest of the day: Whatthehellamidoinghavingababy?

A week later and about four days into our toe ritual, I went in for a routine doctor's visit and he saw that my amniotic fluid was low. This can mean your placenta is conking out and you have to have the baby right away. I had had a completely normal pregnancy up until this time. John had been in New York on a visit and was at the airport to fly back to San Fran. I called him from the doctor's office. "Um, they're saying I might have to have the baby tonight." He got on the phone with the doctor, who told him, "If I were you, I wouldn't get on the plane."

John came back from JFK, skeptical that this was going to be a "thing." By now it was six P.M. and we went to get the ultrasound to get further info. The radiologist came back into the room and said, "Well! You're havin' a baby tonight!"

We'd had a stroke of luck: When I called John to tell him the fluid was low, he was at the gate, and his plane was about to start boarding. Another ten minutes and he would have missed the birth of his son.

This was a month before the baby was due. I hadn't even packed a bag yet. We took a cab back to my apartment, where I frantically threw stuff into a tote bag. Umm, pajamas, some baby clothes to bring him home in, uh, an iPod. John said, "Do you want to bring a book?" "No." I continued my frantic packing. Toothbrush! Phone charger! "You want to bring a book!?" "No." Underwear! Camera! Slippers? "Now you're sure you don't want a book." "I don't know how to make this any clearer—I DON'T READ!" (Sometimes when you are so frantic, you need to boil yourself down to your basic bullet points. Sure, with more time and in calmer circumstances, I may have elaborated that I don't read as often as I'd like, and I fritter away my time on the Internet or watching bad TV. I snapped out "I don't read!" instead, as I certainly couldn't imagine recovering in the hospital as the time I was suddenly going to want to tuck into one of the ol' classics. ("Ms. Dratch, may we check your catheter?" "Hold on. . . . I'm in a particularly riveting chapter of *Middlemarch*.")

We got to the hospital. This was happening whether I was mentally prepared or not, so I could just coast along for the ride, as I had for the whole process. I had buried my head in the sand about all things birth-related. I am supersqueamish about medical stuff and this was the mother lode. I was going to have a C-section because the baby had to come out ASAP. I didn't know this, but if your placenta is failing, it can't sustain through a labor process. The decision had been made for me by circumstance. As I lay there waiting and just hanging out, I could hear the screams and moans of pain from a woman in the next room. "AAAAGGGGHH!" she cried. "AAAAAGGGGG-HHH!!"

Huh. Maybe I was lucky I was escaping from the natural earth-mama way after all.

I was brought into the operating room and was surprised by its stark and clinical quality. I was expecting a delivery room, like with some plaid curtains and maybe a poster of some badly rendered flowers. No. This was an OR. Metal instruments everywhere. Cold. No flower posters, ladies. I'm telling you all this because it's the kind of stuff I always avoid reading. I had tuned it all out.

You get an epidural, which really wasn't bad at all. Nothing hurt, but the anaesthesia makes you really cold, so I was shivering uncontrollably, shaking as if I were having a seizure. Then they lay you down on this table with your arms out in a

Christ pose, throw up a curtain so you can't see your guts out on a table, and start the operation. I kept shaking and shaking and had the worst heartburn I'd ever had in my life. And I could feel a tugging in my guts . . . but nothing truly heinous. John was sitting up near my shoulder, being very sweet. "You're doing great." He also kept telling me to breathe, which is what you tell people who are going through labor. I wanted to tell him to stop telling me to breathe because it had nothing to do with my situation, but all I could bark out was a quick "Sh!" At one point, John stood to readjust his chair. Big mistake. He saw over the curtain—his Viet Nam experience, as he calls it. I've still never asked him what he saw, but I think it was my intestines.

Then we heard it . . . the Cry! The Cry from behind the curtain! It was so sweet and little and high! They brought The Baby, for he was still The Baby until we laid eyes on him, under some heat lamps to work on him because he had a little fluid in his lungs. I couldn't quite see him where they had him, but John could. He looked over and aptly described our son upon seeing him in the first minute of his life. "He's beautiful! . . . He's a charmer!" Even having spotted him for mere seconds and from ten feet away, the fact is, John was exactly right.

Though I waited until the last day in the hospital to fill out the birth certificate, there was one name from my list that John liked as well, and it never lost its number one position, no matter what other names were tossed about. I officially let go of the name Herc, though it will forever have a place as his in utero nickname. My mother's head remained intact. We named our baby Eli.

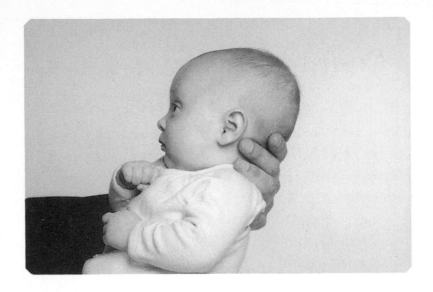

When we were sprung from the hospital, we waited at the elevator with two other couples, who seemed as dazed and clueless as we were. We were all being set free to care for these tiny creatures and just figure this out on our own. Looking at our faces, I wondered how the human race continues to survive.

"Do-It-Yourself Infant Care" or, If You Live Outside Manhattan, "Infant Care"

•—●

I opted not to have a baby nurse when Eli was born. If you live anywhere but New York, you are thinking, "What the hell is a baby nurse? Was something medically wrong with your child?" Well, in Manhattan, it seems like everyone gets a "baby nurse." A baby nurse is someone who is an expert in all things baby and who is there twenty-four hours a day for at least the first two weeks, although more often for a few months if you are really living it up NYC-style. With my one-bedroom apartment, I didn't want to be negotiating around a stranger and a cot during this time. Same with a nanny. Everyone has a nanny here. But without a job to go to, there was really no need, and I wanted my space. I wasn't reporting to a set, where my baby could hang with the nanny while I was off shooting a scene. I was home, and I thought I'd feel weird having a stranger give my baby a bottle while I sat four feet away, nonchalantly watching TV and pounding Doritos. Besides, caring for my newborn was a whole new adventure—I finally had a project, a purpose, a something-to-do!

At this point in my life, I was glad to be doing things this way. If I were younger and still climbing the career ladder, if I hadn't traveled as much yet, if I were still craving the party scene, I might feel differently, but because the baby came so late in the game, I didn't feel torn about staying with him all the time. The big slowdown of my career, which initially felt like such a curse, actually felt quite fortunate now. I could truly say: "See that, Hollywood!? Mwah hah hah haaa! I'm the winner here! I get to stay here with my baby all day if I want to, all day, every day, and not leave him with my staff or a nanny. I don't have to leave the house at six A.M. and get back at all hours of the evening. I get to be here day after day and not miss a moment! What's that, Hollywood? You don't care? Oh yeah? . . . Well . . . OK. Well. You just . . . you! . . . OK, forget it."

John and I figured out everything as we went along—fascinating stuff like belly button maintenance, proper burping, and bottle sterilizing. If I had doubts about my child-care abilities, I'd think of teen mothers to make myself feel better. (There are sixteen-year-olds doing this on MTV! Surely, I can do it!) Without any outside help, there were definitely times when I was totally overwhelmed by all of my own little tasks that needed a couple minutes. I didn't understand before I had a baby that, except when they are asleep, you have *no* time to do anything. I don't mean time for luxurious things like reading a magazine or talking on the phone or cooking yourself dinner. (We ordered delivery on a nightly basis for about six months, I believe.) I mean you don't have time for such basic things as taking out the garbage or doing the dishes or taking a shower. Until he was about four months old and could roll over, Eli lay on a little pillow and watched me take a shower every day, so he may be scarred for life.

Eli was so tiny and delicate and sweet. At the beginning, I checked him obsessively as he slept in the bassinet next to the bed. "What are you doing?" John would whisper.

"I'm just checking him."

"He's *fine*," came the voice from the darkness.

"Well, I'm a Neurotic Jew!" I retorted.

"Well, take it easy, N.J."

One night, John was asleep and I crept over to Eli, trying to make out his figure in the bassinet and just make sure he was breathing. I crept back silently into the bed, thinking my check went unnoticed. Two seconds later, I heard a whisper from half-asleep John.

"What's going on, N.J.?"

Busted.

I was never getting more than four hours of sleep straight for a stretch, if that, and this went on for two or three months, yet everyone said I was glowing. I *felt* like I was glowing. The *SNL* schedule was perfect training for motherhood; I was used to crazy nighttime hours. Being awake at three in the morning, in the dead of night when the streets are pretty quiet, didn't feel at all weird to me. It actually felt quite normal. And I was fortunate enough to avoid the 'mones that make you crazy and sad after giving birth. If anything, I was feeling euphoric. Sure, I had a few meltdowns when I could not get Eli to sleep after trying for hours. One morning at around five A.M., when Eli was about two months old, I was sobbing, walking around the apartment with him screaming and me just saying, "Please go to sleeeeep."

ELI: *Waaaaaaah.*
ME: *Sob. Sniffle. Snort.*
ELI: *Waaaaaaah.*
ME: *Waaaaaaah.*
ELI: *Waaaaaaah.*
BOTH OF US IN UNISON: *WAAAAAAAH!*

Actually, this very incident cemented the fact for me that I am a horrible dramatic actor. Later that day, I had an audition for the show *Nurse Jackie* in front of the director, who, for this episode, happened to be Steve Buscemi. Having just spent the very early hours of the morning crying with frustration because Eli wouldn't sleep, I had to go in and audition to play a mom who is crying in frustration because her kids are driving her crazy. I had just had pretty much the *exact* experience in real life that morning, yet when faced with replicating it in an acting situation, I tanked it hard. I could hear myself reciting the lines, not being the character at all. While I was reading the lines, simultaneously a voice was sounding in my head, literally saying the words "*Get out of the business. Get out of the business.*" Because I respect Steve Buscemi so much, I was embarrassed to the point that I now think of that as the Worst Audition of My Life. As an actor, I can say that the only good thing about the Worst Audition of Your Life is you can pretty much be sure another one will come along to knock it out of first position, sometime in the not-so-distant future.

My only other case of extreme hormones after the birth was when I cried because I missed one of my favorite TV shows. To make the pain even worse, I realized that I only *thought* I had missed it and then, when I turned on the TV, discovered I could have been watching it for the whole hour. That's when I started to cry, at the realization of my grave error. John was there to witness my crying breakdown. I knew I was being ridiculous, but that did not stop the tears and half laughing, half sincere whimpering that was happening. The show I had missed? *RuPaul's Drag Race.* Some may relax with a warm bath, their favorite music, or a foot rub from a loved one; I had had a particularly exhausting day of child care, and that night I just really needed my drag queens.

First Comes Love, Then Comes Marriage, Then Comes the Baby in the Baby Carriage

●—●

When I was in my late thirties, I felt somewhat ashamed that I wasn't married. I had always imagined myself married. Everyone I had grown up with was married. All my friends from college, with the exception of some gay men, were married. I felt I had somehow missed the boat. Then my baby worries took precedence over marriage worries. When I realized I had cheated the whole system and would have a baby without a marriage, I no longer cared about marriage. This great anxiety lifted from me. I didn't have a time clock and I was going to have a baby and if love were meant to happen, it could happen whenever on its own time. Marriage started to seem like a silly social convention to me. Then I found myself in the position

where the man I had been casually dating was going to be seeing me attached to a breast pump on a regular basis. At this
point, marriage made a lot more sense to me. If you have any
desire to have a man stay by your side and he's going to see you
hooked up to a breast pump, you should probably be bound by
a legal contract.

This brings me to the point of trying to be in any way
seductive postbirth. Now, some women may go on and on
about the natural beauty of womanhood and the lush feminin-
ity of their wonderful life-giving bodies, blah blah blah. I
could see that idea maybe applying when you are with someone with whom you have a history: your passionate years, your
romantic getaways, your deep and soulful conversations by
candlelight, your seeing each other through some hard
times—all adding up to a beautiful tapestry that culminates in
the creation of a new being who is a testament to your love for
each other. When that man looks at the body of that lady, it is
a reflection of all the love and shared times. Then there is getting knocked up by the guy you have known for six months,
and trying to still be in any kind of flirtation phase when you
are hooked up to a breast pump that makes you look like the
Titty Monster from Outer Space.

Let me elaborate. If you have never seen a breast pump, to
say that it is "not sexy" would be a gross understatement. There
are two plastic funnels that go over the nipples. Each funnel is
connected to a bottle to collect the milk. The funnel also has a
tube connected to it that leads to the mechanism that creates
the vacuum pump that works your nipple, stretching it long
into the funnel with each pump. Are you turned on yet?

In addition, there is also a hands-free bra so you can go about your business, a bra with holes cut out where the nipples are, so the whole kit and caboodle is attached to your body through this medieval device. Now imagine that you didn't already have a big romantic phase on which your husband can draw if he cares to block out your current status. And you are in your current status for a large portion of the day. In spite of my aforementioned huge jugs, I wasn't producing a lot of milk. The solution to this problem is that you are supposed to pump eight times a day for fifteen minutes. That doesn't sound so bad until you realize that is TWO HOURS out of your day, on top of the time you are feeding the baby, which is already occupying much of your day. Eight times a day of pumping when you are operating on no sleep, and as soon as the baby goes to sleep, you just want to sleep too but instead, there you are, hooked up like Ol' Bessie.

During the pregnancy too, I had to let go of all vanity—what little I had—and was just glad I was having a baby. In the third trimester, I developed the only really negative pregnancy symptom that I got the whole time, and that was wicked heartburn. I'd never had heartburn and didn't know what it really even was, but now I was saddled with it. There were so many foods I couldn't eat that I was eating healthier than I ever had—no pizza, no sugar, nothing greasy—and even if I wanted to have a glass of wine on occasion, I couldn't because of the heartburn. On a nightly basis, I'd bolt up from bed, tapping myself on the sternum to try to relieve the pain. I would create odd burps and squiggly noises, the kind that should be saved for after an exchange of *I love you*s and planning for a future together. Because of the squawks emanating from me, John started calling me The Pterodactyl. Not Lambkins, not Cuddlebuns, not Snuggie-wuggie, but Pterodactyl. One night, the second after I turned the lights off, I let out a huge burp. I started laughing uncontrollably. I didn't mean to do it. That became the Shot in the Dark. I don't even want to tell you about the Axis of Evil. That was the time I burped and farted at the same time. I'm not a public farter, lifting a leg and saying, "Get a loada this one!" I was mortified.

Once Eli was born, there were days when I was so busy with baby care that I wouldn't even go outside or have any contact with society. One day around three P.M., I was finally venturing out of the apartment to go for a walk with John. On the elevator, John happened to glance down and said, "Are your pants on backward?"

"Huh?"

I looked down and realized that in my haste in the morning, I had slipped my maternity jeans on backward at six A.M. and hadn't noticed all day long. The moment vanity officially leaves your life is when you look down to discover an asslike configuration living where your front pockets should be.

I know new moms aren't thinking about how they look, caring for a baby 24/7. I was no exception, but remember, I still had one foot in an odd courtship phase. My worst moment in this regard was one day when I stumbled out of the bedroom, hair wild and unkempt, completely naked except for a My Breast Friend nursing pillow, which is sort of a foam flying saucer that straps around your waist. Half asleep, I stumbled out to go to the bathroom. I looked up and saw John sitting in the living room. I think he must have felt the way the guy did who took that famous picture of Bigfoot frozen mid-stride. I looked like a feral child who had emerged from the forest.

We silently met eyes and I went on my way, back into the woods, having just had an odd encounter with civilization.

It's not easy to keep any mystique alive, caring for a baby in the midst of the courtship phase. In an instant, the makeup comes off, the pants are on backward, and you find that on a daily basis, you are walking the Earth in the form of your inner Sasquatch.

The Natalie Merchant Converse Axiom of Child Care

●–●

Let me explain what it's like having a baby in New York City. You know that Natalie Merchant song "What's the Matter Here?" It's about child abuse and how she sees a woman abusing her child and she wants to speak up about it, but she doesn't dare say anything. *"And I want... to say...'What's the matter here?' But I don't dare saaayyyyy 'What's the matter here?'"*

Having a baby in NYC is the opposite of that song in every way. . . . You are *not* abusing your child and everyone *does* dare say "What's the matter here?" Complete and utter strangers. Sure, if you were doing something truly bad, everyone would go about their business because of the fear of breaking social convention, but why oh why does every New Yorker—and they are almost always women—feel the need to tell you your child is going to be "TOO COLD!!" I can't tell you how many times

I've had to explain to a complete stranger on my elevator that I bundle Eli up downstairs in the lobby because he fusses too much if I put warm clothes and a hat on him in my apartment. I do a preemptive speech to stop these darn nosy New Yorkers from their oh-so-not-helpful child-care advice. I didn't start out with the speeches; they developed as a response because every time I would get on the elevator, someone felt it was their civic duty to say "It's cold out there!" while looking at the baby. I started to develop retorts in my head. *"Oh yeah?"* I would fire back silently in my mind. *"Well, did you know that in Iceland they leave their babies outside in the cold because they think it's good for their health?!"*

One day when I was particularly fatigued, I got on the elevator and a woman said, "He's going to be too cold out there!" because I hadn't put his gear on yet. I just nodded, the postpartum hormones and three hours of sleep filling me with the rage of a grizzly bear. Then she said, "And his *shoe* is coming off!"

First of all, babies don't need shoes. They don't walk. Their feet don't touch the ground. Shoes are just for decoration. Second, he was going to be under a sleeping bag doohickey once I got him in the lobby. When this woman said, "And his *shoe* is coming off!" I almost turned into an active volcano and spewed hot lava from my mouth. I felt the words about to snarl out of me in huge black cartoon letters and pummel her to the ground: "WELL, WHY DON'T YOU CALL CHILD PROTECTIVE SERVICES?"

I was really glad I didn't say that, because at the time I didn't think she lived in my building, but I saw her the next day on the elevator and that would have been awkward.

The Natalie Merchant Converse Axiom also applies very much to sleep, specifically to a segment of society I came to know as the Sleep Shamers. For some reason, the first question out of everyone's mouth to ask about your baby is "How's he sleeping?"

"Ohhh! He's so cute! IS HE SLEEPING?"

"So you had a baby! *HOW DOES HE SLEEP?*"

"Baby!baby!baby!baby!SLEEP????"

I don't know how to answer. Um . . . Lying down with his eyes closed?

Sleep is an area in which moms can really rev up their egos to full mast and feel like they know what you should be doing. I have found that, for some reason, this is particularly true of the whole "Cry it out" School of Moms, or Ferberizers (named for Dr. Ferber, who invented the "Yer on yer own, kid" system of sleep instruction).

I just knew in my heart I was not a Ferberizer. Luckily, in Babyland you can pretty much find any school of thought that matches yours and just say, "I'm going with this guy." For me, that happened to be Dr. Sears. He's the "attachment parenting" guy who says, "Don't cry it out, carry your baby on a sling with you for closeness, and breast-feed whenever they want, and it's even OK to have them sleep in your bed with proper precautions." Because I found I was doing much of this anyway, I just thought, "OK, well, Dr. Sears says it's all right, so I'm down with it."

If you don't cry it out, you will find that this is *not* OK with the Ferberizers. I don't mean it's not OK for *their* kids, which it's not, but it's also not OK with them that someone *else*'s kids, even a complete stranger's kids, aren't being Ferberized. They *really really* want you to make your baby cry it out too. It's important to their souls. If your kid cries it out, they will get enough sleep to be a successful and productive human being, go on to Harvard, and become the CEO of their own company and a generally revered member of the community. If your child doesn't cry it out or get the requisite eleven hours, they will have ADD and not get into the right preschool, thereby setting them on a path of failing grades, early juvenile delinquency, and a meth addiction culminating in a tristate murder spree.

I find an odd correlation—another converse axiom, if you will. The Ferberizers that *I* have met are not breast-feeders. The same woman who will barrage me with the benefits of the eleven-hours assured sleep and a life of sleep freedom will say about breast-feeding, "Oh, I was not going to do that! Uh-huh! I wanted no part of it!" Now, do *I* turn around and say in a scolding tone, "Well, you gotta take one for the team on this, Judy! I mean, you *have* to breast-feed! Don't you know that *studies show meow meow meow IQ points meow meow immune system meow meow meow*"? No. I don't.

All moms secretly think they are doing *something* wrong and there's *something* that slipped through the cracks, so I guess when some women think they are doing something *right*, they want to shout it at you from the highest mountain. I picture them standing on the playground, holding a megaphone, and proclaiming to all who will listen:

"I MADE MY OWN BABY FOOD TODAY! MASHED POTA-
TOES WITH RICOTTA AND ORGANIC CHIVES! IT WAS
BETTER THAN WHAT I ATE MYSELF!"

"AVA SLEEPS TWELVE HOURS A NIGHT—*IN* THE CRIB,
NO ROCKING, *NO* SLEEP SHEEP . . . BOO-YA!"

"MAXIMILLIAN'S HEAD CIRCUMFERENCE IS IN THE
90TH PERCENTILE!" "Is that good?" "I DON'T KNOW! BUT
IT'S THE 90TH PERCENTILE!!"

Eli sleeps pretty well as far as I can tell, but I haven't been around other babies, so what the hell do I know? If I had to wake up and be alert enough to argue a case in court or do brain surgery or be a senator or, hell, make the fries at McDonald's, then yeah, maybe I'd take drastic measures like Ferberizing too. For me, though I work here and there, for the most part I'm a cavewoman, a primitive example of motherhood. I stay home and take care of the baby. I have a man to hunt and gather for me if I need it (though I can often be spotted at Trader Joe's). But for now, I'm enjoying my time as a cavewoman. And I think cavewomen went to their babies at night when they cried. Actually, I'm betting cavewomen were the original "co-sleepers" so the baby was right there anyway, not off in some "cave nursery" with little furniture and choo-choo trains on the walls. What I'm saying is, I don't think cavewomen Ferberized. Of course, they also lived to age thirty and didn't brush their teeth. But still.

Over Theeeere! Over Theeeere!

●–●

My father has absconded with the baby again.

We are walking down the High Line in Chelsea. My dad loves manning the stroller. He is so into manning the stroller and gazing at his grandson that sometimes he breaks into a rapid pace, forgetting his surroundings and the surrounding party of people who are also there to bask in the light of the Glorious Manchild. These fugitive runs tend to coincide with cases of extreme temperature. Right now, it is nearing ninety with bright sun. The last time he went on the lam like this, we were in Vermont for Thanksgiving. Dad took Eli for a walk in the stroller in the dead of winter, and my mom had to chase him down in the car a mile away. This was John's first big family experience with me, so he got to witness a lifetime of family dynamics enacted on a dirt road in Charlotte, Vermont. Having tracked her subject like Dog the Bounty Hunter, my mother slows down the big, embarrassing red Caddy and rolls down the window in the winter air.

"PAUL! What are you doing?!"

My dad is keeping up the brisk pace, singing songs to Eli in the frigid weather. Eli is bundled up, but his hands aren't under the blanket and they are cold. The ladies in my elevator would have had a field day.

"PAUL!"

"We're on a walk!" he says cheerily.

"PAUL! Get in the car!"

The marching continues. "I'll walk back! We're having fun. He's having a blast!"

"Paul, it's freezing out! Get in the car now!!"

John looks over to my brother, who for some reason got roped into this hunt for the obsessed grandfather. To my brother, my mother telling my dad what to do and my dad off on an enthusiastic-bordering-on-madcap tear is old hat. John's just seeing this now, as his son is rolled along through the New England winter, possibly, if left unchecked, past the Canadian border.

My brother looks at John and just shrugs, rolling his eyes as if to say, "What can ya do?"

My dad grudgingly hands Eli over. Eli's hands get warmed up. They come back to the house—where I've been waiting—blustering in from the cold.

"Ahhhhh, I love this little guy! We had so much fun!" Eli got a good dose of the Icelandic Plan for Good Baby Health that day, courtesy of Paul Dratch.

Now, at the High Line, in the summer heat, we have to chase my dad down the path, but he's way ahead of us. He disappeared from sight long ago. We catch up to him finally and he brightly reports, "We're having a blast! Aw, look at him. He's my little buddy!"

He's oblivious to the fact that once again, he's been hogging the baby.

My parents not only came around to the idea of the pregnancy and grandchild, they have been reborn. They come to New York at least once a month. Every time my father visits, at some point in the weekend, he will take me aside, look at me very seriously, lower his voice, and say, "You have given us such a blessing" or "He's such a miracle." Only with his Boston accent, it sounds like "He's such a merracle." He'll bust into the apartment saying, "Where's my little buddy?" and "Ohhh, I love this little guy so much!" My dad puts on a real show for Eli, always singing or marching him around or pointing out trees and flowers. My mom is the more quiet one, but Eli appreciates her as well in a very sweet way. She'll just be sitting there on the couch and he'll crawl over and look up and flash one of his smiles especially for her. She'll look down and laugh. "Oh, hello!"

A weird phenomenon is that when my parents are around Eli, they become about one hundred times more Jewish than they are in real life. My dad will start singing as if he just walked off the boat from the Old Country—great hits like "Yaidle deedle dai, yaidle deedle dee . . ." and its B side, "Deedle yaidle dai, deedle yaidle dai." My dad grew up in an immigrant household, where his parents spoke Yiddish. My mom, on the other hand, is second generation and did not grow up speaking Yiddish. You wouldn't know this, though, when she is dealing with Eli. "Oh, look at that little punim!" "Come here, little butchkie." "Hello, bubbele." Once she said, "Ohhh, you little fresser," a word I'd never even heard before, and I said, "Mom! Who are you?" Eli was making them tap into some primal ancestral lore or something mysterious. They both started channeling the songs and language that may have been sung and spoken to them when they were babies. When my dad would bust into some really Yiddish song, I'd start to get a bit self-conscious around John, imagining him thinking, "What the hell are they saying to my child?"

"Dad, could you change up the repertoire?" I'd say.

"Huh? OK. Too Jewish?" And he'd switch over to war songs. Again, I guess these were the songs he associated with being a kid. Of *course* a baby wants to hear war songs. It's only natural.

So while other grandparents are softly crooning "Rock-a-bye Baby" or "Twinkle, Twinkle, Little Star," my father is careening down the sidewalks of New York, pushing the stroller, not taking his eyes off the little "merracle." He enthusiastically belts out another tune that in his world is perfect for a baby: *"FROM THE HALLS OF MONTEZUMA, TO THE SHORES OF TRIP-OLIIIII! WE WILL FIGHT OUR COUNTRY'S BATTLES OVER LAND AND AIR AND SEA . . ."*

The family is in hot pursuit.

The Great Pile of Unknowns

●—●

Back when I was pregnant and John had gotten used to the idea of fatherhood, he started to think of all the fun things he could do with a son. He fantasized about taking his son to games, throwing the ball around, and going fishing—all the traditional father/son activities. He also mentioned a family heirloom of sorts that he was excited to pass down to Eli. When John was a kid, his mother had taken a ceramics class and had painted a little statuette for him. The statuette was of a baseball player, and John's mom had even personalized it by inscribing *To John, 1975, Love, Mom* on the bottom of the player's foot. John thought of how cool it would be to write *Eli* with the date on the other foot . . . a true sentimental father-to-son family heirloom.

John excitedly approached me when it arrived in the mail. "My mom sent the statue for Eli!" He unveiled it to me. There was a little fact he had left out in the telling: The statue was creepy as hell.

I blurted it out instantly. "That's creepy." The thing looked like Chucky.

"No! It's cute!" said John.

To me, the young lad had evil clown elements—wide-set impish eyes and a too-broad smile that put me in mind of a maniacal ventriloquist's doll. What kind of psychological damage could be done to my son by going to bed under the demonic eyes of this boyish baseball player who, I was betting, came to life at night and ran around the room in a crab walk?

John left it on the table in my living room. The eyes would follow my every move. I couldn't live with this statue in my realm. I was afraid I might roll over in bed and the thing would be lying next to me, staring at me with his enormous grin and wide-set eyes. John took the statue back to his place and we

put it on the list of "things we would deal with later."

There were a lot of things on this list. Things we didn't even talk about as things on the list. Where would Eli go if we simultaneously kicked the bucket? No idea. Hadn't been discussed. How would we explain our unique situation to Eli? Who knew what we would even *be* by the time such a discussion came up? You may be thinking, "Well, *I* would have discussed these things," but we were focusing on how well we were doing for two people thrown into a big situation and how much worse things could be if either one of us had turned out to be difficult, uncompromising, or a stone-cold freak.

In dealing with the "now" of infant care, many what-about-down-the-roads got shelved for a time when we were actually down the road. Of course I would have loved to have everything in its place mentally and emotionally for Eli's sake. But Eli's appearance on the scene was unique and I didn't question my good fortune in having him come into my life. He wasn't by the book to start with, which was his magic, and I hoped we could focus on that magic and go with the flow. So heavy topics got pushed to another day. We hadn't even discussed religion.

I would like to raise Eli Jewish or at least have him learn about Judaism, not because I'm superreligious but because I feel a cultural and historical obligation to pass down the traditions. You can't really pick up what Judaism is all about without making some effort with religious school. John had no knowledge of Judaism at all. I'm not even sure he had met many Jewish people in his life. The only Judaism I exposed him to thus far was a seder for Passover thrown by a friend of mine here in New York City, when Eli was about seven months old. It was a very casual affair, each couple who was attending consisting of a Jew and a non-Jew. Looking around, I realized I was the most learned Jewish person in the room, which is not saying a lot. Woe to the people if I were the one entrusted to know enough about Judaism to be the expert. You realize how little you know about your own religion when you are asked to explain it to a newbie.

John asked me, "So what is it we're going to?"

"It's a seder."

"What is it? What do we do?"

"It celebrates when the Jews escaped from Egypt. It's just like a dinner party, only there are little readings throughout."

"Wait. Am I going to have to read something?"

"Yeah, but don't worry about it. Everyone reads a little part. It's not a big deal."

"We have dinner, but people are reading during it? So . . . it's like a murder mystery?"

Pause. "Yeah. It's like a murder mystery."

When pressed for details about everything and I heard myself explaining my religion, I realized I may as well have been describing the Swahili creation myth. That is how random this stuff sounded coming out of my mouth.

"Passover is the celebration of the Jews getting out of Egypt. And there's this plate of symbolic foods on the table and we explain what the foods mean. Like there's the bitter herbs that you dip in salt water that represent the bitterness of our plight and the tears." My mind started racing about how John was going to react to various parts of the seder. "We open the door so Elijah the Prophet can come in, and we leave a cup of wine for him." I may as well have been saying, "Oh, and we wait for a ghost to come in and have a drink too." What about the Ten Plagues? That could be a problem. "See, we list the Ten Plagues that God sent down upon the ancient Egyptians, and you put a drop of wine on your plate for each plague." I started thinking of how weird it was going to be when he is at this dinner party and we start saying in unison, "Vermin!" "Boils!" and "the Slaying of the Firstborn!" If I were happening upon someone's religion for the first time, and everyone were tossing around the phrase "the Slaying of the Firstborn," I may well have made a mental note on the location of the exits. I mean, how the hell am I going to sell John on my religion? I wish the Jews had had better PR people when all the traditions were getting started. Didn't they know what they'd be up against? Santa Claus and Christmas trees and caroling and eggnog? Easter bunnies and baskets of chocolate? And what are we offering? . . .

"No, seriously, get on board with me here. Happy Yom Kippur, y'all! And now comes the part where we don't eat all day. We *fast*! Isn't that fun?"

Or "You think you'd like an Easter basket full of candy, boys and girls? Nooo. You're Jewish! How about some dry unleavened bread topped with a delicious dollop of horseradish! Gather 'round, kids!! Mmmm!"

I have my work cut out for me, but for now it's on the "later" pile with the creepy statue. I care more about the religion issue than the creepy statue, but the pile's pretty big, so there's room for dilemmas large and small.

Addendum: After I wrote about the creepy statue and photographed it for a visual aid, John accidentally knocked him off his perch and he shattered into four pieces. I actually do feel bad about that, like I may have put a curse on the little guy. I'm hoping he can be glued back together so Eli can have this family heirloom in his possession, passed down lovingly from generation to generation. And so he can learn early on the signs of what creepy people look like.

"You May Ask Yourself..."

●—●

Perhaps the biggest question on the pile of the Unknown is "What's up with you and John?" I get asked it almost every day. It's even knocked the "What happened with *30 Rock*?" question out of top position. Good friends to mere acquaintances ask, and I don't really have a pat answer. How do I introduce John to people? I feel weird just saying simply, "This is John." I feel like I should say, "This is my baby daddy, John." "This is my boyfriend, John." Maybe "This is John, a-guy-I-was-casually-dating-long-distance-and-then-surprise!-I-became-pregnant-and-we-are-figuring-it-out-and-he's-involved-as-a-father-but-we're-not-sure-what-our-relationship-is-going-to-be. Nice to meet you!"

Sometimes, to make myself feel normal, I imagine that we are from India and are in an arranged marriage, and how statistics show that arranged marriages have an equal success rate to "soul mate" marriages. "If only I were Indian," I'd think, "my situation would be totally ordinary!"

In those moments when our "courting personae" would go

out the window and give way to our inner Bigfoot, John and I discovered that we have a fundamental difference of style, along with the obvious East Coast/Midwest, actor/business-man, or flaming liberal/possible secret Republican divisions between us. I guess the best way to describe our different styles (now that I can fully cop to the fact that I am an airy-fairy hippie-dippie person) is that he is an Earth sign and I am a Water sign. From my scanty knowledge of horoscopes, that means, for example, I'm fine with arriving at an airport with minimal time as opposed to wanting to hunker down and get coffee and read the paper at the gate for two hours. (Now, granted, I have missed two planes in my life and he's probably missed none.) John's apartment is neat and tidy, and mine, well—one time early on, when John was coming to visit, I said I had to clean my apartment before he came over.

He said not to bother.

"Don't bother?" I said. "But I want to."

To which John replied, "I've seen your apartment and I know how you live, Sanford and Son."

And if, say, I'm walking around my apartment holding Eli, and I notice that my ass crack has been exposed because my pants are falling down, I don't give it that much thought. Who cares? I'm holding a baby. John prefers order—order of time, space, and, I found, order of pants being at your waist and not an inch or two down your crack. If he says, "Hey, the plumber's here!" or worse yet, "Pull your pants up," it makes me insane. . . . I have had minimal sleep, and I've been immersed in Baby-land for the whole day, and I'm not exactly looking for Glamour Don'ts. You may as well just throw one of those black strips across my eyes for the next three years. When John makes such comments, I tell him that I want to dropkick him into the center of a circle of suburban moms so they can rip into him like a pack of hyenas. Ladies, can I get a what-what?

Though he denies it, sometimes I feel he would rather be with a woman who shops at Talbot's and wears a headband and pearls and always has aspirin on hand in a delicate pillbox that she carries in her fresh, square Coach bag. Looks like the Casting Directors on high ended up going in a Different Direction.

Maybe there's a middle ground, though. I have to admit, last time John gave me the side-eye over my wardrobe choice, a ratty red shirt that I wear on an every-other-day basis under a red sweatshirt, I got really annoyed with him and marched off to the Duane Reade drugstore to run my errands, whereupon an older lady passing me in the aisle immediately asked if I worked there.

In spite of the challenges our Earth/Water energies can present, what I never foresaw is that John plays a very different role for Eli than I do. John is all about physical play—stuff it wouldn't cross my mind to do. He's always riding Eli on his shoulders like he's in a horse race, or moving his legs around back and forth until Eli is in a laughing fit as John says his own invented chant of "Shake 'n Bake! Shake 'n Bake! What's my favorite chicken?" Though I am supposed to be the comedian in the family, it's John who often gets him laughing in a crazy baby belly-laugh giggle fit. I'm the Regulator—time to nap, time to eat, time to change the diaper, time for a bath, but Eli knows that when John walks into the room, here comes the fun! (I discovered from talking to other moms that's a common dynamic—so unfair!)

When Eli was born, our lives each took a dramatic turn, albeit a delightful, joyful turn. However, our former lives as single people out on the town were a mere several months in our past, fading away in the rearview mirror. Sometimes, John and I catch ourselves in a stereotypical mommy/daddy scenario, like taking a car ride with the car seat, the diaper bag, all the gear. Perhaps Eli has just projectile-vomited in the backseat and we are cleaning it all up and surrounded by rags, sippy cups, and formula. In times like this, we would bust out a tiny fragment of a line from the Talking Heads song "Once in a Lifetime." You know, the line that goes *You may ask yourself . . . how did I get here?*" One of us would simply say in a David Byrne voice: "You may ask yourself . . ." It seemed to provide relief by putting a needed twist on the most domestic of situations.

Since bringing Eli home, I've had many moments when I've looked down at myself as if in an out-of-body experience as I walked him in the stroller, in complete wonderment that this was my life. It seemed possible I would wake up and realize this had just been a really detailed and elaborate dream. My brain *still* isn't used to the miracle—I had it so hardwired to be anti-miracle. I would guess because of this fact, I am extra-appreciative and don't mind at all the sleep deprivation, the time deprivation, and the sudden absence of cavorting late at night, Montepulciano, and expertly made tagliatelle Bolognese.

Once Eli first started smiling at around two months, no matter how early it was, no matter how little sleep I'd gotten, and no matter how much I have never in my life been a morning person, I'd look over and see him smiling away, and my inner monologue would go instantly from "Oh God, I'm so exhausted—what the hell time is it—what the . . . ?" to "Awwww, you little guy. You got me again!"

I know. I know. I'm sounding dangerously like one of the Baby Shower People—talking about sleep schedules and breast pumps and, now, how cute my baby is. If you are anything like Former Me, you may be reading this and thinking, "OK, so she became one of those Shower People. Now I have to hear stories about how great life is with a baby and how cute his poops are." I know the feeling.

I remember one Sunday afternoon, long before Eli, long before John. I was in my early forties and had that low-level single-lady panic revving quietly about where my life had ended up as opposed to where I thought it would be. I went to join a friend for lunch. He was with one of his good friends, a beautiful, successful actress whom I had met a few times through him. She was also in her early forties, though she was married to a dreamy guy and was the mother of a new baby. When I walked up to the table, she bluntly said to me, "You look depressed!" This chick barely knew me. Now, either she was extremely rude and presumptuous or she was seeing through my own self-denial into my core. I still don't know which. It was a Sunday, and Sunday Feeling can be mistaken for depression, or I suppose Sunday Feeling can straight-up *be* depression.

As lunch progressed, they were chatting about this and that. Famous Actress had rubbed me the wrong way or jarred my soul—again, I can't say which, maybe a combo platter of both—and I was having trouble getting back on the rails into the conversation. Then she said, "I know what will cheer you up! You should come over sometime and just hang out with the baby! That'll cheer anyone up!"

I wish I had a freeze-frame of my face the second she said that. I'm sure an anthropologist studying the microexpressions of my eyes, my mouth, and every single muscle in my face would conclude that that particular combination of muscular reactions equaled the universal response of "BITCH, PLEASE."

OK, Shower People, listen up. *WHY* would a single lady in her forties, with no prospects and, at this point, no hope in her heart want to go spend her time at a *beautiful* actress's house— which I'm sure is designed and decorated like something out of a magazine, for I'd heard she had *impeccable* taste—and willingly, I mean VOLUNTARILY, walk into Perfectville to spend time with Perfect Baby? *That* is going to cheer me up? Does a person on a strict diet go hang out at Ben & Jerry's all day and look at people eating sundaes to "cheer up"?

Single Ladies, Former Me's, Trouble Conceivings, Gay Men Wondering, and the two Straight Men who are concerned about having a child in a timely fashion—I know babies can be a delicate topic, because I lived on the other side for so long. If a baby is something you are struggling about, I would just say, don't be like I was and let your fears dictate your future. I think I would have been too scared to explore what my other options were if I hadn't had the divine intervention of the Hawaiian Volcano gods. Because I have found that having a baby in your life is pretty wonderful. I have to be honest about that. However, I also solemnly promise to not e-mail you baby pictures and talk about the Cutest Poop Ever. I've been there. I lived it. And I know—you don't need that shit.

So . . . I hate to not be able to tie everything up in a neat little bow, but right now my story doesn't really have an ending. As for John and me, sometimes it feels like we are boyfriend and girlfriend. Sometimes it feels like we are co-parents. Sometimes it feels like we are newlyweds with a newborn. Sometimes it feels like we are a couple of bickering eighty-year-olds who have been together for years. I understand from talking to my married friends with babies, all of these roles fall within the normal range of parenting an infant. I guess if I had to pick the most apt description, I'd say it mostly feels like we are platoon buddies. There we are, lying in the dark, having fought the good fight all day long. . . .

"Hey, Michigan, you awake?"

"Barely. What is it?"

"Michigan, you miss your old life back home?"

"What's that, New York?"

"I says, you miss your old life back home?"

"Aw, shaddup and get some sleep, New York—what's the point of thinking about it?"

"C'mon, Michigan, you must miss it—the trees, the quiet, comin' and goin' as you please. Not answerin' to nobody . . ."

"Aww, get some shut-eye, New York . . ."

"Well?"

"Yeah, sometimes I miss it. I wonder what I'm doin' here on the front lines—changing diapers, livin' on Third Avenue with the loud traffic and the NYU students and the whatnot, but maybe this is where I'm s'posed to be. . . . Life's funny, ain't it?"

"Sure is, Michigan."

Sound of a garbage truck outside. A horn honks for forty seconds.

"What about you, New York?"

"Huh?"

"You miss your old life?"

"Ahh. Not really."

"Aw, go on, New York—you don't miss it? The glitz? The glamour? The shrimp cocktail? The cocaine parties?"

"Nah."

"Bein' on live TV on Saturday nights? Rubbin' elbows with Lorne Michaels and Steve Martin and Jimmy Eat World?"

"Are they a band?"

"Yeah, they played on the show."

"Oh. I can't remember some of these newer bands."

"How 'bout Bruce Springsteen and Mick Jagger and Sting?"

"Yeah, those were some cool times."

"How 'bout Will Ferrell and Maya and Ana and ol' Parnsy?"

"Yeah, I miss the fellas. . . . *What was that?*"

"It's just the sirens from Beth Israel."

"Oh. OK. I get so jumpy out here on four hours of sleep a night."

"I know, New York. So do ya miss it?"

"You know what, Michigan? Yeah, I miss it sometimes, but

I had the experiences, and that's enough for me. I wouldn't trade Eli for an Emmy or a WGA or even a SAG award."

"That's good to know. What about an Oscar?"

"Nope. Not for an Oscar."

"Good. 'Cause that would be some fucked-up shit. Trading your baby for an Oscar."

"Did you just say the F-word, Michigan?"

"Yeah. I guess I did."

"Well, I guess we ain't so different after all."

"I guess not, New York. I guess not."

"Good night."

"Good night."

"Sweet dreams."

"Sweet dreams."

Ten seconds pass.

"*WAAAAAAAAH! WAAAAAAAAH! WAAAAAAAAH!*"

"Are you gonna get him, New York?"

"Yup . . . I'll get him."

"*WAAAAAAAAAAAAAAAAAAAAAAAAAAAAAAAAAAAAAH!*"

Epilogue

I feel that the kind of work I was doing before this new job I have as a mom will eventually come around again. I'd love to do a comedy on Broadway at some point, and more TV. I'd love to do a funny part in a film, maybe in a kind of indie film that goes to Sundance and then gets released into the wider world. (Did I just put that out there into the *Universe*?!) For now, though, I'm enjoying all my free time to spend on what I had stopped imagining I might ever have. People will say to me, "So are you taking a hiatus from work to spend time with the baby?" and I say, "Uh . . . yeah . . . let's call it a hiatus. That's it. I'm taking a hiatus, by choice!"

And, luckily, my agent still calls now and then. Next time he calls, though, I'm not going to be surprised. I'll know what to expect. I think it might go like this:

RRRIIIING RRRIIIING!

"Scott! What's up?"

"Hey, Rachel. Got an offer for you. Now, I'm gonna warn

you, just hear me out 'cause I don't know if you're gonna wanna do it."

"Yeah?"

"It's the part of Marta . . ."

"OK, this already sounds like a fat person."

"Yeah, well, it says in the script she's obese, but—"

"I can just put my own spin on it."

"Yeah, they want your spin. Now, you'd be playing Amy Poehler's mother. . . ."

"Are you joking?"

"No."

"Anyway, Amy, Tina, and Maya are starring in this film. They are playing superheroes. The script is fantastic. It looks like it's gonna be huge."

"I'm sure it will."

"And they want you to do a walk-on as Amy's mother."

"Yeah?"

"Yeah. Still listening?"

"Yup."

"Now, Amy's mother is from a mutant planet, so you're not only obese but you're a mutant."

"So would it be, like, prosthetics or special effects?"

"No, no, no. It's just you. You're playing the mutant just on your own, no special makeup. With your spin on it. They like your facial expressions."

"OK, I'm going to choose to take that as a compliment."

"Oh, and also—"

"She's a lesbian?"

"Yeah! On her planet, everyone's a lesbian. You're Amy Poehler's mutant lesbian mother."

"OK."

"OK what?"

"OK, I'll do it."

"You will?"

"Yeah, I'll do it."

"I thought you said you wanted to get away from these kinds of parts."

"I do."

"So why are you doing it?"

"Well, if Hollywood sees me as an obese sixty-five-year-old lesbian mutant from another planet, then I guess that's what I'll be. I'll just be laughing all the way to the bank."

"It pays scale."

"Really?"

"Yeah. 'Cause they kind of thought you might want to work with your friends, but if you don't want to do it, they're just going to give it to an unknown."

"OK."

"OK what?"

"I'll still do it."

"You're sure?"

"Yeah."

"I thought you were gonna turn this one down."

"Yeah, I would have before, but what the hell. I'm a trained and experienced comic actor! And I *think* I can be the best and funniest obese lesbian mutant the world has ever seen. Plus, you know what they say! Work begets work, right? THAT'S WHAT THEY SAY! BLARGH!"

"What was that?"

"Oh, nothing. I was just practicing a mutant voice."

"Oh! You scared me! Sounds good! OK, well, I'll let them know."

"BYYYEEEE! THIS IS MARTA SIGNING OFF! MARTA THE MUTANT!"

"Bye, Rachel."

"Bye."

I will hang up the phone. I will put Eli into the BabyBjörn and walk over to the swings. As I walk with him against me, I will hold each of his little bare feet in each of my hands, swinging his legs as we go. I have his meaty feet on the palms of my hands and I play with his tiny toes.

There is no better feeling.

Acknowledgments

Thank you to my literary agent, Lydia Wills, for the first push, for always insisting on referring to me as a "writer," and for far too much to name after that. Thanks also to my editors, Jessica Sindler and Lauren Marino, for their invaluable second opinions every step of the way. And thanks to Scott Metzger for being my agent as well as my cheerleader.

Huge, huge mega-thanks to Ryan Shiraki and Megan Davis Collins for sharing the wise insights of the true writers they are

ACKNOWLEDGMENTS

and the unlimited availability of the true friends they continue to be. I'd also like to acknowledge David Beach, Irene Bremis, Susan Williamson, and Catherine Burns for helping me when I needed an outside ear in the home stretch.

Thanks to Piccolo Café for letting me write this book there.

I'm eternally grateful to Lorne Michaels for giving me my big break, and also, Lorne, thanks for sending me flowers in the hospital after the birth! I don't know if anyone's told you this before, Lorne, but you're a class act. Thanks to Mary Ellen Matthews, Tom Broecker, Eric Justian, Dana Edelson, and Kelly Leonard for helping with the book cover and with gathering photos. Also thanks to Hal Willner, Sheila Rogers, and Claire Mercuri for helping me get to Billy Joel, and to Mr. Joel for allowing me to reprint his breakdown-inducing lyrics.

To my brother, Dan, for being my first comedy partner, and to the Lexington Ladies for being my first unofficial improv group from elementary school onward. And heartfelt thanks to my parents, Elaine and Paul Dratch, for never telling me any aspiration was too crazy to pursue.

Finally, to John, thank you for your caring devotion to our son, for trusting me with our story, and last but not least, thank you for your turbo-sperm.